CW01548247

Pouring Water on Time
A Bilingual Topical Anthology
of Classical Arabic Poetry

Other Books by Gerlach Press:

THE CALIPHATE AND ISLAMIC STATEHOOD
FORMATION, FRAGMENTATION AND MODERN INTERPRETATION
Edited and Introduced by Carool Kersten
3 Volume Set
883 pages
ISBN: 978-3-940924-52-0

SADIK J. AL-AZM
SECULARISM, FUNDAMENTALISM
AND THE STRUGGLE FOR THE MEANING OF ISLAM
Collected Essays on Politics and Religion
With a Foreword by Stefan Wild
3 Volume Set
627 pages
ISBN: 978-3-940924-20-9

SADIK J. AL-AZM
CRITIQUE OF RELIGIOUS THOUGHT
First Authorized English Edition of Naqd al-Fikr ad-Dini
With a New Foreword by the Author
Translated from the Arabic
by George Stergios and Mansour Ajami
240 pages
ISBN: 978-3-940924-44-5

AZIZ AL-AZMEH
THE ARABS AND ISLAM IN LATE ANTIQUITY
A Critique of Approaches to Arabic Sources
168 pages
ISBN: 978-3-940924-42-1

www.gerlach-press.de

Mansour Ajami

Pouring Water on Time
A Bilingual Topical Anthology of Classical Arabic Poetry

With a Foreword by Sadik J. Al-Azm

Gerlach Press

First published 2016
by Gerlach Press
Berlin, Germany
www.gerlach-press.de

Cover Design: www.brandnewdesign.de, Hamburg
Printed and bound in Germany by Hubert & Co, Göttingen
www.hubertundco.de

© Gerlach Press 2016 and the Author
All rights reserved. No part of this publication may be reprinted or reproduced, or utilised in any form or by any electronic, mechanical, or other means, now known or hereafter invented, including photocopying and recording, or in any other information storage or retrieval system, without permission in writing from the publisher.

British Library Cataloguing in Publication Data.
A catalogue record for this book is available from the British Library.

Bibliographic data available from Deutsche Nationalbibliothek
http://d-nb.info/1082374164

ISBN: 978-3-940924-74-2 (hardcover)
ISBN: 978-3-940924-75-9 (ebook)

Contents

Foreword *by Sadik J. Al-Azm* ix

Introduction 1

On Generosity 21

On Life 28

On Time and Days 32

On Gray Hair and Youth 38

On The Length of a Lover's Night 47

On Love-Induced Emaciation 51

On Love 59

On Soul-Melting Love 73

On Ṣūfī Love 76

On the Phantom of the Beloved 78

On Wine and Drinking 82

On Beauty 88

On Soft Skin 93

On Eyes and Tears 99

Carpe Diem 105

On Poetry and Meaning 107

On Grief 110

On Awe 112

On Separation 115

On Jealousy 117

It was as though I ***poured water on time***
when I unsheathed hope,
a sharp sword,
to protect him
against time

Abū Tammām (d.231/845)

Acknowledgements

I owe profound gratitude and appreciation to my wife, Barbara, who indefatigably, objectively, and patiently (with occasional explosions) read, proofread, and edited the manuscript. I am also greatly indebted to my friend, the Lebanese poet and editor Tony Shasha, for his extraordinary ability and great care in producing a grammatically accurate manuscript of the Arabic text, complete with vocalization, desinential inflection, prosody, and diacritical markings.

I am most thankful for both of them for their remarkable help and perseverance. I am also most appreciative of the encouragement and assistance given me by professors Alexander Key of Stanford University, Rebecca Gould of Yale University, and Lara Harb of Dartmouth College. And finally, I am utterly grateful to my esteemed professor of philosophy, Dr. Sadik J. Al-Azm, who read the manuscript with a discerning critical sensibility and insight.

Transcriptions

Arabic words or geographical names where spelled are as in the Oxford Dictionary. To improve reading fluency, proper names were spelled as they usually appear in the English language press and publications. If these names, especially geographical names, are less familiar or may be confusing, the detailed transcription will be given in parentheses when the word is first mentioned.

If Arabic words could not be found in the Oxford Dictionary, I used the transcription used by the US library of Congress. Foreign language words other than proper nouns or geographical names were italicized. (Download: http://archimedes.fas.harvard.edu/mdh/lcromanization.pdf [last access 10 April 2015])

The Library of Congress transliteration system is employed with easily recognizable minor modifications. The definite article is retained throughout except where there is elision or a metrical necessity in cited verses. Then *al* is governed by the ensuing “sun” or “moon” letters.

Foreword

For Mansour Ajami, Arabic poetry is that Midas touch which transmutes the most commonplace words, the most mundane meanings and the most pedestrian images into the shimmering gold of the poetically soaring and sublime. This is what he calls "the alchemy of glory," sublimating the earthly language, truth and meaning of daily life into poetry's glorious languages, into poetry's luminous meanings and its noble truths. Thus, when poetry pours its alchemical waters over worldly time it washes away the timeliness of time to give us the timeless.

Ajami's exquisite critical introduction to this topical bilingual anthology of classical Arabic poetry, spanning eight centuries, brings to the fore the debates, squabbles and controversies of classical Arabic literary critics and theoreticians concerning the dialectics of the "true" and the "false" in poetry and their relevance to devices like license, latitude, hyperbole, exaggeration, excess, extravagance, simile, metaphor and so on.

This anthology is topical, presenting the best of Arabic classical poetry's musings over the many faceted states of the human condition, among them love, generosity, life, time, youth, beauty, ecstasy, longing, wine, death and plenty more. Ajami's selection of the topical verses and poems was guided by what was deemed best in its genre by the quasi consensus of the great classical Arab literary critics and theoreticians.

Ajami is reputed for his superb literary translations from Arabic into English, and I dare claim some of his renderings could almost work as English literature. His equal mastery of the source language and of the target language and his talent and skill in moving seamlessly back and forth between the two languages have all reached their peak in this anthology.

All lovers of poetry, specialists in comparative literature, multicultural literary enthusiasts, translators of Arabic literature into European languages, sensitive Middle Eastern area studies experts, and students of the Arabic language and of its history and culture will all find a great deal to satisfy, edify and enrich them in this extraordinary volume.

Sadik J. Al-Azm — Berlin, Spring 2016

Introduction

Medieval Arabic literary critical thought engendered three binary dialectical oppositions: the first, *al-Lafẓ wa-'l-Maʿnā* (phraseology and meaning, also translated as form and content; sound and sense or substance);[1] the second, al-*Maṭbūʿ wa-'l-Maṣnūʿ* or *al-Ṭabʿ wa-'l-Ṣanʿah* (natural and artificial poetry, also translated as spontaneous, unaffected, as opposed to affected, mannered poetry);[2] and the third, *al-Ṣidq wa-'l-Kadhib* (truthfulness and untruthfulness, or truth and falsehood or lying).[3]

The third literary dualism, *al-Ṣidq wa-'l-Kadhib* (truthfulness and untruthfulness), embodied its dialectic in three oppositional terms: firstly, the best poetry is the most truthful (*aḥsanu 'l-shiʿri aṣdaquhu*); secondly, the best poetry is the most untruthful (*aḥsanu 'l-shiʿri akdhabuhu* or *aḥsanuhu akdhabuhu*); and thirdly, the best poetry is the most moderate (*aḥsanu 'l-shiʿri aqṣaduhu*).

Critics and literary historians, and to a certain extent philosophers, employed the issue of truthfulness and untruthfulness as a criterion for the selectability, preference, comparison, often to determine plagiarism, and interpretation of the "best" verses composed on various topics or themes. A poet's degree of compliance with or divergence from the "classical norm," the method of the early Arabs, the canonical rules of poetry *('amūd al-shiʿr)*, was verified through the poet's moderate or excessive employment of hyperbole, exaggeration, lying, or of figurative metaphorical expression in general.

The critics' deft utilization of some of the finest samples of Arabic poetry to resolve the dialectic of truth and falsehood evinces at once an inspired, enthusiastic aesthetic of poetry and a refined method of practical criticism, and establishes the singularity and endurance of those celebrated verses.

1. Medieval Arab critics, literay historians, philologists and grammarians discussed this essential literary issue of phraseology and meaning extensively and methodically. For a survey of the issue, See my Ph.D. dissertation, *Al-Marzūqī's Treatment of ʿAmūd al-Shiʿr* (The Essentials of Poetry), Columbia University in New York City (1976).

2. The issue of spontaneous or mannered style was discussed by Mansour Ajami in a critical study entitled *The Neckveins of Winter*, E.J. Brill (Leiden, 1984). It will be referred to in this introduction.

3. The dialectic of the issue of truthfulness and untruthfulness was examined in a critical monograph, *The Alchemy of Glory: The Dialectic of Truthfulness and Untruthfulness in Medieval Arabic Literary Criticism*, Three Continents Press (Washington, D.C., 1988), by Mansour Ajami. Extensive reference will be made to that book in this introduction.

Medieval Arabic poetry is characterized by the linear progression of the short poem or the longer ode (*qaṣīdah*). The polythematic poem, structurally mono-metered and mono-rhymed, was in actuality a congeries of lines strung together like the "pearls of a necklace", with at least one line emerging as the central piece (*wāsiṭat al-ʿIqd*) or piece de resistance of the poem. Occasionally, two or more lines, especially in the rare case of enjambment, would become prominent, but an essential principal verse, the quintessence of the poem, would stand out as the *bayt 'l-qaṣīd* of the whole poem. The single two-hemistich line in such a scheme was independent, epigrammatic, viable, and transposable, embodying the meaning, the "meaning of meaning", the "image of meaning", and any literary conceit or phraseological embellishment. As such, the single verse presented an optimal sample of a unit of reading; the poem was simply a vehicle for the disparate, discrete, self-sustained lines themselves.

Almost paradigmatically, medieval philologists, critics, literary historians, and philosophically oriented critics generally selected, interpreted, compared and made preferences among such single verses, not whole poems. Many of those choicest lines became famous, acquired the universal currency of proverbs, and have been extensively quoted to the present time. The single two-hemistich line has thus become the universe of poetry, the nucleus around which both the poem and medieval critical thought coalesced.[4]

The exacting necessity of the mono-rhyme scheme in the mono-metered poem invariably led to copious padding, superfluity, and digression. It fostered factual or fabulously exaggerated descriptions, as in panegyric and satire, deterministic philosophical aphorisms, or gnomic, didactic verses, often overladen with phraseological affectation, syntactical compression, linguistic and rhetorical mannerisms and flourishes, or mere indulgence in "uncouth" (*ḥūshī*; unfamiliar) and erroneous (*sāqiṭ*) words. That chiefly obtained in compliance with the necessities of meter and rhyme."[5] What was left, therefore, was a line or a few lines of poetic excellence, "best" lines, in a whole poem.

The poet, composing within the definitive, rigid, stultifying structure of the poem, could, in the opinion of some critics, be moderate (*yaqtaṣid*) in description, comparison, panegyric, or invective poetry. The poet could also exaggerate (*yubāligh*) or be immoderate (*yusrif*) so that his discourse corresponded to or resembled the absurd (*al-muḥāl*). However,

---

4. Bashshār ibn Burd (d.167/784) was asked who was the best poet ever. He replied that he was, contending that he had written at least one thousand poems with at least one prominent quotable line in each poem. That, he claimed, made him the "best" poet. Medieval Arab poets commonly made such preposterous claims and each pompously and foolishly considered himself to be the best poet.

5. Ḥāzim al-Qarṭajannī, *Minhāj al-Bulaghā' wa-Sirāj al-Udabā'*, Ed. Muḥammad al-Ḥabīb ibn al-Khūjah, Dār al-Kutub al-Sharqiyyah (Tunis, 1966), pp. 81- 82, and Mansour Ajami, *The Alchemy of Glory: The Dialectic of Truthfulness and Truthfulness in Medieval Arabic Literary Criticism*, Three Continents Press (Washingto D.C., 1988), p. 111.

immoderation (*al-saraf*), untruthfulness (*al-kadhib*, lying), and absurdity (*al-muḥāl*) were not appreciated in any form of discourse except in poetry.[6]

In expressing his poetic meanings—ideas, concepts, motives, connotations, etc., the poet therefore could either resort to hyperbole, exaggeration, or he could adopt an intermediate course. The critics preferred hyperbole as the better of the two options.[7] Poets who opted for hyperbole merely sought exaggeration (*mubālaghah*) and added emphasis. But by projecting the magnitude, omnipotence, omnipresence of a patron or a described object, exaggeration became a criterion of poetic superiority. Thus, al-Ḥazīn al-Kinānī's (n.d.) line:

Yughḍī ḥayā'an wa-yughḍā min mahābatihi
fa-mā yukallamu illā ḥīna yabtasimu

He casts down his eyes in modesty
Others cast down theirs in awe
And so he can be spoken to
only when he is smiling

is inferior to a line by Abū Nuwās (d.198/814 or ca. 200/815) in the same meaning: [8]

Wa-akhafta ahla 'sh-shirki ḥattā annahu
la-takhāfuka 'n-nuṭafu 'l-latī lam tukhlaqi

You have so frightened the polytheists
that even their unborn embryos
are afraid of you

Poets who employed exaggeration and hyperbole that surpassed the realm of the "positive" (existent, *mawjūd*) to that of the "privative" (non-existent, *ma'dūm*) intended their poetry to be metaphorical, a *mathal* (a figurative expression)[9] and their descriptions to be the

6. See Ibn Wahb al-Kātib (Isḥāq ibn Ibrāhīm), *al-Burhān fī Wujūh al-Bayān*, Eds. Aḥmad Maṭlūb and Khadījah al-Ḥadīthī (Baghdad, 1967), p. 185, and *The Alchemy of Glory*, p. 24. Ibn Wahb corroborates his own stance on poetry, granting it more legitimacy, by stating that Aristotle had described poetry as containing more lies than truth (*al-Kadhibu fīhi aktharu mina 'l-ṣidq*). Aristotle also stated that lying is permissible in poetic composition (Ibid. p. 24). Qudāmah ibn Ja'far (d.337/948) also stated that the best poetry is the most untruthful, commensurate with the Greek philosophers' conception of poetic language, *Naqd al-Shi'r*, Ed. S.A. Bonebakker, E.J. Brill (Leiden, 1956), p. 26, and *The Alchemy of Glory*, p. 21.

7. See Qudāmah ibn Ja'far, *Naqd al-Shi'r*, Op.Cit., p. 26, also *The Alchemy of Glory*, pp. 20-21. *Ma'na* (meaning) as a calque also means significance; subject; subject-matter; denotation; connotation; motif; sense; essence; theme, image etc. depending on text and context.

8. *Naqd al-Shi'r*, P. 27 and *The Alchemy of Glory*, pp. 21-22.

9. "*Mathal*" also means: analogue; "old" metaphor; prototype; likeness by comparison; conceit; proverb, maxim; parable; example etc. For the various meanings of "*mathal*" and "*tamthīl*", see Helmut Ritter's

ultimate in poetic excellence. This course was considered to be better than the moderate course.[10] More explicitly, what is intended of hyperbole, a "good quality of meaning", is exaggeration, *tamthīl* (topical representation; the application of a *mathal* to a given topic), intensity of action, emphasis, and not the conveyance of the true nature of the described object.[11] However, the poet ought to avoid two major defects of meaning: impossibility and contradiction (*al-istiḥālah wa-'l-tanāquḍ*) in the employment of hyperbole. Such a defect obtains when a *mumtani*ʿ (impossible but not inconceivable) meaning is ushered into the realm of the possible or the existent. The *mumtani*ʿ is that which "does not exist in reality, but which can be imagined by the mind", such as attaching the paw of a lion to a man.[12]

The contradictory (*al-mutanāqiḍ*) and the impossible, on the other hand, "neither exist nor can they be conceived by the mind". An example of a *mumtani*ʿ meaning treated as something possible is the following line by Abū Nuwās:

Yā Amīna 'l-lāhi ʿish abadan
dum ʿalā 'l-ayyāmi wa-'z-zamani

O Amīn 'l-Lāh! May you live forever
and endure as long as there are
days and time

The poet in this line has "surpassed the confines (*ḥadd*) of hyperbole (*ghuluw*), which can possibly occur, into the domain of the *mumtani*ʿ (impossible but not inconceivable) which cannot possibly occur. Hyperbole indeed surpasses the essence and inherent characteristics of the described object to that which cannot possibly occur to it."[13] And as long as the poet refrains from entering the impossible-but-not-inconceivable (*al-mumtani*ʿ) into the realm of the possible and refrains from employing impossible and contradictory meanings, hyperbole is sanctioned and appreciated.

The critic and literary historian Abū Hilāl al-ʿAskarī (d. 395/1004) defined hyperbole as equivalent to impossibility or absurdity, and not merely as a legitimate "expansion" of meaning. "Hyperbole exceeds the limits of a meaning and elevates it to an almost inaccessible end." An instance of such hyperbole is the following verse in which the poet depicts the hostile stares of enemies:

---

introduction to his edition of ʿAbd al-Qāhir al-Jurjānī 's *Asrār al-Balāghah*, Istanbul Government Press (Istanbul, 1954), pp.11-16, and Wolfhart Heinrichs *The Hand of The Northwind*, Deutsche Morgenlandische Gesellschaft, Steiner (Wiesbaden, 1977), pp. 6, 7 ff.

10. *Naqd al-Shiʿr*, p. 27, and *The Alchemy of Glory*, p. 21

11. *Naqd al-Shiʿr*, p. 31, and *The Alchemy of Glory*, p. 22.

12. See al-Qarṭājannī, *Minhāj al-Bulaghā'*, p. 76, and *The Alchemy of Glory*, p. 107.

13. See *Naqd al-Shiʿr*, p. 132, and *The Alchemy of Glory*, p. 23.

Yataqāraḍūna idhā 'ltaqaw fī mawṭinin
naẓaran yuzīlu mawāṭi'a 'l-aqdāmi

They exchange,
whenever and wherever they meet,
stares that obliterate
each other's footprints

Or this line by al-Aʿshā (d. 7/629):

Fatan law yunādī 'sh-shamsa alqat qināʿahā
awi 'l-qamara 's-sārī la-alqā 'l-maqālida

What a chivalrous youth he is!
Were he to sit in company
with the sun
the sun would cast its veil,
Or with the journeying moon
the moon would drop its reins [14]

A farfetched form of exaggeration is characterized by some critics as a "repose (*istirāḥah*) for the poet: whenever he is incapable of producing a good meaning, he exaggerates. Thus he preoccupies the listeners with what is absurd (muḥāl) and at the same time he awes them."[15] In contrast, accessible exaggeration employed to "complete" (*tatmīm*) a meaning or an image, which may appear as agreeable padding (*ḥashū*), is deemed an acceptable form of exaggeration. An example of such exaggeration is Ibn al-Muʿtazz's (d. 296/908) verse describing his horses:[16]

Ṣababnā ʿalayhā ẓālimīna siyāṭanā
wa-ṭārat bihā aydin sirāʿun wa-arjulu

We poured our whips harshly on them
until their swift fore and hind legs
flew away with them

14 See Abū Hilāl al-ʿAskarī, *Kitāb al-ṣināʿatayn: al-Kitābah wa-'l-Shiʿr*, Eds. ʿAlī M. al-Bijāwī and M. Abū 'l-Faḍl Ibrāhīm, ʿĪsā al-Bābī al-ḥalabī wa-Shurakāh, 2nd edition (Cairo, 1971), pp. 369, 372, and *The Alchemy of Glory*, p. 44.

15. See Ibn Rashīq al-Qayrawānī, *al-ʿUmdah fī Maḥāsin al-Shiʿr wa-Ādābih wa-Naqdih*, Ed. Muḥyiddīn ʿAbd al-Ḥamīd, 4th edition, 2 vols., Dār al-Jīl (Beirut, 1972), vol. 2, p. 54, and *The Alchemy of Glory*, p. 71.

16. See Ibn Rashīq, *al-ʿUmdah*, Op.Cit., p. 54 and *The Alchemy of Glory*, p. 71.

In addition to "expansion" and "completion" of a meaning or an image, Ibn Rashīq (d. 456/1063 or 463/1070) characterized the "exhaustion" (*taqaṣṣī*) of a meaning in order to attain the utmost possible description of an object as one of the "best and most extraordinary types of exaggeration: ʿAmr ibn al-Ayham's (n.d.) line is an example:

> *Wa-nukrimu jāranā mā dāma fīnā*
> *wa-nutbiʿuhu 'l-karāmata ḥaythu kāna*
>
> We honor our neighbor
> as long as he is with us
> And we follow him
> with our generosity
> wherever he goes

The poet thus "exhausted" whatever description of his tribe's bounty he was capable of expressing poetically. In sum, moderate exaggeration that utilizes such good elements of speech as metaphor and simile, and that fully consummates a meaning is acceptable, agreeable and necessary, for if exaggeration is abolished or censured then both metaphor and simile are abolished and censured , as also would be other qualities of good speech.[17] On the other hand, immoderate, farfetched exaggeration and its two variants, over-exaggeration (*ighrāq*) and extravagant excess (*ifrāṭ*), is discredited by Ibn Rashīq and other traditionalist Arab critics. The following line by al-Aʿshā is termed excessive by Ibn Rashīq:

> *Fa-law anna mā abqayti minnī muʿallaqun*
> *bi-ʿūdi thumāmin mā ta'awwada ʿūduhā*
>
> If what you have left of me
> were hung from a stalk
> of panic-grass
> the stalk would not bend

In essence, Ibn Rashīq places moderate exaggeration over truthful expression and argues that if a poet is inclined to *ifrāṭ* (extravagant excess; excessiveness), he should use it sparingly, with no more than one line in a poem, and should not make a practice of it.[18]

Another critic, al-Khafājī (d. 466/1073), offered an approach that treats moderation in both exaggeration and hyperbole as a reflection of poetic skill. If hyperbole inclines towards what is "impossible", then it is censured, but if it inclines towards what "approximates the

17. See Ibn Rashīq, *al-ʿUmdah*, p. 55 and *The Alchemy of Glory*, pp. 71-72.

18. See Ibn Rashīq, *al-ʿUmdah*, pp. 60, 61, 64, and *The Alchemy of Glory*, P.74.

truth" then it is commendable.[19] In this context, Abū Nuwās' line is faulted because of its "hyperbolic and extravagant excess (*ifrāṭ*) that exceeds the truth":

Wa-akhafta ahla 'sh-shirki ḥattā annahu
la-takhāfuka 'n-nuṭafu 'l-latī lam tukhlaqi

You have so frightened the polytheists
that even their unborn embryos
are afraid of you.[20]

Al-Khafājī further asserts that poetry is structured on license and latitude-- useful elements for accommodating farfetched, immoderate hyperbole. One such reliable stylistic device is the employment of the words *kāda, yakādu, takādu*, (almost, nearly, all but), or *law, wa-law, k'anna* (if; even if; as if), and similar words, which the poets have traditionally used. The employment of the words *kāda* (preterite verb, almost) and *yakādu, takādu* (aorist verb, almost) prevents the meaning from entering into the unacceptable domain of the impossible or contradictory. Thus, the verb *Kāda*, or its imperfect *yakādu, takādu*, should be employed in exaggerated hyperbolic statements so that poetic discourse can be "closer to the domain of truth,"[21] can attain proximity to the realm of the possible,[22] and can enhance the verse's accessibility. Examples of such tempering usage are the famous following lines by al-Buḥturī (d. 284/897), al-Mutanabbī (d. 354/965) and Abū Ṣakhr al-Hudhalī (d. 2nd half of 7th century) respectively:[23]

Atāka 'r-rabīʿu 't-ṭalqu yakhtālu ḍāḥikan
mina 'l-ḥusni ḥattā kāda an yatakallama

Cheerful spring has arrived,
strutting about,
laughing with beauty,
until it almost talked.

****

Yuṭammʿu 't-ṭayra fīhim ṭūla aklihimu
ḥattā takāda ʿalā aḥyā'ihim taqaʿu

19. Ibn Sinān al-Khafājī, *Sirr al-Faṣāḥah*, Ed. ʿAbd al-Mutaʿāl(i) al-Saʿīdī, 2nd. Edition (Cairo, 1969), p. 280, and *The Alchemy of Glory*, p. 79.

20. *Sirr al-Faṣāḥah*, p. 263, and *The Alchemy of Glory*, p. 80.

21. *Sirr al-Faṣāḥah*, p. 263; *al-ʿUmdah*, vol. 2, p. 64; *Naqd al-Shiʿr*, p. 133; and *The Alchemy of Glory*, pp. 23 and 80.

22. Ibn al-Athīr, Ḍiyā' al-Dīn, *al-Mathal al-Sā'ir fī Adab 'l-Kātib wa-'l-Shāʿir*, Eds. Aḥmad al-Ḥūfī and Badawī Ṭabānah, 4 volumes, Maktabat Nahḍat Miṣr (Cairo, 1959-1962), vol.3, p.194, and *The Alchemy of Glory*, p. 84.

23. *Sirr al-Faṣāḥah*, p. 263, and *The Alchemy of Glory*, p. 80.

The vultures are so covetous of them
for their long feasting
on the bodies of their enemies
that they almost alight
upon the living amongst them

****

Takādu yadī tandā idhā mā lamastuhā
wa-yanbutu fī aʿrāqihā 'l-waraqu 'n-naḍru

My hand almost becomes dewy
when I touch her
and green leaves sprout
on its fingertips

A more intensive case of still commendable (*mustaḥsan*) exaggeration, even though the poet's "immoderation" entered the meaning into the realm of "untruthfulness and absurdity" (*al-kadhib wa-'l-muḥāl*), are the following lines by Abū Nuwās:

Fa-law tus'ali 'l-ayyāmu mā 'smī mā darat
wa-ayna makānī mā ʿarafna makānī
Taghaṭṭaytu min dahrī bi-ẓilli janāḥihi
fa-ʿaynī tarā dahrī wa-laysa yarānī

If the days were asked about my name
they would not know who I am
and about my abode
they would not know where I live
I shielded myself from my fate
with the shadow of its wings
so my eyes see my fate
but fate sees me not [24]

The use of exaggeration (*mubālaghah*) without *kāda* (almost) but with similar "commendable" effects is exemplified by the following lines by al-Maʿarrī (d. 449/1057), al-Namir ibn Tawlab (N.d.), and al-Nābighah (d. 604 A.D.) respectively:[25]

24. Ibn Wahb al-Kātib, *al-Burhān fī Wujūh 'l-Bayān*, Op.Cit., pp. 185-186, and *The Alchemy of Glory*, p. 25 "*Fa-law tus'ali 'l-ayyāmu*" can also be read as "*fa-law tas'ali 'l-ayyāma*" (were you to ask the days).

25. *Sirr al-Faṣāḥah*, pp. 264-265, and *The Alchemy of Glory*, pp. 80-81.

Wa-nabbālatin min Buḥturin law taʿammadū
bi-laylin anāsiyya 'n-nawāẓiri lam yukhṭū

If even at night
the archers of Buḥtur
were to aim at the pupils
of their [enemies'] eyes
They would not miss

****

Al-Namir ibn Tawlab, describing an old sword to which he compares himself:

Taẓallu taḥfiru ʿanhu in ḍarabta bihi
baʿda 'dh-dhirāʿayni wa-'s-sāqayni wa-'l-hādī

You would still have to search
for it in the ground
after you have struck arms,
legs, and necks with it

and al-Nābighah:

Wa-lā ʿayba fīhim ghayra anna suyūfahum
bi-hinna fulūlun min qirāʿi 'l-katā'ibi

There is no fault in them
but that their sword-blades
are notched from striking
mailed squadrons

The poet may even exaggerate in his descriptions to the degree of attaining the absurd (*muḥāl*), some of which could be received as excellent facetiae (*nawādir*) and bons mots. An example of such witty exaggeration are the following lines by al-Mu'ammal ibn Amyal (n.d.):[26]

Man ra'ā mithla ḥibbatī
tushbihu 'l-badra in badā
Tadkhulu 'l-yawma thumma tad-
khulu ardāfuhā ghadā

---

26. See al-Āmidī, Abū 'l-Qāsim al-Ḥasan ibn Bishr, *al-Muwāzanah Bayn Shiʿr Abī Tammām wa-'l-Buḥturī*, Ed. Aḥmad Ṣaqr, 2 vols., Dār al-Maʿārif (Cairo, 1961, 1965), Vol. 1, p. 156, and *The Alchemy of Glory*, pp.32, 38.

Who has ever seen anyone
like my beloved
who resembles the full moon
when she appears
If she enters the house today
her buttocks will follow
tomorrow

and al-Nābighah's (d. 604) line:

Idhā 'rtaʿathat khāfa 'l-jabānu 'rtiʿāthahā
wa-man yuʿallaq ḥaythu ʿulliqa yafraqi

Were she to wear earrings
the cowardly earrings
would fear
Verily, whoever dangles
from where they are
would certainly show fear

In the same vein, description intended for derision, disparagement or ridicule can be appropriate, even though it "leads to impossibility (*iḥālah*, absurdity)", in Ḥāzim al-Qarṭājannī's (d. 684/1285) judgment, as in the following line by al-Ṭirimmāḥ (d. ca.105/ 723):[27]

Wa-law anna burghūthan ʿalā ẓahri qamlatin
yakurru ʿalā ṣaffay Tamīmin la-wallati

If a flea on the back of a louse
were to charge against
the ranks of [Banū] Tamīm
They would flee

However, "absurdity" that obtains as truth, according to al-Āmidī (d. 370/980), is more repugnant than absurdity that is occasioned by "exaggeration (*mubālaghah*) and expansion of meaning." Al-Āmidī cites the following line by Abū Tammām (d. 231/845) as being both:

Bi-yawmin ka-ṭūli 'd-dahri fī ʿarḍi mithlihi
wa-wajdiya min hādhā wa-hādhāka aṭwalu

A day the length
and width of time

27. See al-Qarṭājannī, *Minhāj al-Bulaghā'*, p. 134, and *The Alchemy of Glory*, p. 116.

But my grief is longer
than both

Abū Tammām accorded width to time which al-Āmidī declared to be "purely absurd." It is superfluous, he added, to borrow "width" for time, because the poet had already completed the meaning by mentioning its "length" and had thus achieved the purpose of the exaggeration. Furthermore, al-Āmidī rejected the interpretation of this exaggeration as an "expansion of meaning or as a metaphorical expression" on the grounds that the words "length," "width," and "time" are lexically formulated as "truth" terms and are categorically not metaphorical. Truth cannot be metaphorical, al-Āmidī averred.[28]

Like truth statements, some philosophically untruthful statements are not poetic. An untruthful statement such as I drank the sea or I carried the mountain; an impossible (absurd, *muḥāl*) statement such as I shall visit you yesterday or I visited you tomorrow; an impossible meaning that cannot possibly exist such as the world is an egg; or a meaning that is both untruthful and impossible such as I saw a man standing and sitting, or sleeping and awake; all such untruthful statements cannot be poetic.[29]

In contrast, untruthful meanings that are conceivable are permissible, acceptable, and poetic, as most poetry is based on untruthfulness and impossible-but-not-inconceivable descriptions.[30] However, actual truth can be transformed into poetic truth: "If an actual truth statement were transformed metaphorically, then it would be called poetry or a poetic statement and it would have the effect (fiʿl) of poetry." An example of metaphorically transformed poetry are the following lines by Kuthayyir ʿAzzah (d. 105/723):

Fa-lammā qaḍaynā min Minan kulla ḥājatin
wa-massaḥa bi-'l-arkāni man huwa māsiḥu
[Wa-shuddat ʿalā hudbi 'l-mahārī riḥālunā
wa-lā yanẓuru 'l-ghādī 'l-ladhī huwa rā'iḥu]
Akhadhnā bi-aṭrāfi 'l-aḥādīthi baynanā
wa-sālat bi-aʿnāqi 'l-maṭiyyi 'l-abāṭiḥu

28. See *al-Muwāzanah Bayn Shiʿr Abī Tammām wa-'l-Buḥturī*, vol. 1, pp. 196-197, and *The Alchemy of Glory*, pp. 32-33. Al-Āmidī devoted seven long pages (197-203) to a semantic, logical refutation of this line, quoting copiously from other poets and from Abū Tammām himself on the diverse, conventional uses of these terms. This kind of systematic detailed analysis, though rather rare in medieval Arabic literary criticism, demonstrates further the significance of the single line, not the whole poem, as a poetic unit for the "selection" and "preference" of the "best" poetry on a particular topic.

29. See *Kitāb al-Ṣināʿatayn*, p. 76, and *The Alchemy of Glory*, pp. 41-42.

30. See *Kitāb al-Ṣināʿatyn*, p. 142, and *The Alchemy of Glory*, p. 42. In a similar context, Al-ʿAskarī related the following anecdote: A poet was asked, "You claim that you do not lie in your poetry, yet you said, 'Indeed, you are braver than a lion.' Is it possible for a man to be braver than a lion?" The poet replied: It is possible, for we have seen Majza'ah ibn Thawr [the poet's patron] conquer a city, but we have yet to see a lion do that". Ibid., p. 245.

When we had performed
all our duties at Minā
And whoever wished to touch
the sacred corners [of the Kaʿbah]
had done so
[And when our saddlebags were strapped
to the humpbacked dromedaries
and the early-comer would not notice
the late-comer]
We began to exchange tidbits of conversation
while the ravines flowed
with the necks
of our mounts

Ibn Rushd (d. 456/1063 or 463/1070) stated that these verses became poetry by virtue of the poet's employment of the image in the last line: "We began to exchange … while the ravines flowed with the necks of our mounts," instead of his merely saying: we rode and talked.

A similarly metaphorically transformed meaning is the following celebrated image:

baʿīdatu mahwā 'l-qurṭi

Deep is the abyss
below her earrings

This hemistich became poetry because of the cleverly employed metaphor. The poet, ʿUmar ibn Ābī Rabīʿah (d. 93/712), borrowed "*mahwā*" ("abyss") to describe the distance between a woman's ears and her shoulders. If he had merely wished to state a fact, he would have simply said: "She has a long neck".[31]

The alchemic transformational power of poetry can, according to ʿAbd al-Q̲āhir al-Jurjānī (d. 471/1078),"create, out of ignoble material, inventions (*bidaʿ*) of transcendental value," especially in the genres of panegyric and satire (lampooning; invective poetry). The following "excellent" lines by Ibn Sukkarah (d. 385/995) attest to the "elixir" of poetry, ʿAbd al-Q̲āhir al-Jurjānī enthusiastically ascertained:

Wa-'sh-shi'ru nārun bi-lā dukhānin
wa-lil-qawāfī ruqan laṭīfah
Law hujiya 'l-misku wa-hwa ahlun
li-kulli madḥin la-ṣāra jīfah

---

31. See Ibn Rushd, Abū 'l-Walīd, *Talkhīṣ Kitāb Arisṭūṭālīs fī 'l-Shiʿr (al-Sharḥ al-Wasīṭ)*, in *Fann 'l-Shiʿr*. Ed. ʿAbd al-Raḥmān Badawī, 2nd. Edition, Dār al-Thaqāfah (Beirut, 1973), pp. 242-243, and *The Alchemy of Glory*, p. 60. A woman's long neck is a feature of great beauty in medieval Arab culture.

Kam min thaqīli 'l-maḥalli sāmin
hawat bihi aḥrufun khafīfah

Poetry is fire without smoke
and rhymes are subtle spells
Were musk, worthy of all praise,
to be satirized by poetry,
it would become a corpse
How many a noble man
of high estate
has been toppled by
light-hearted verse.[32]

Another transformed truth that excited ʿAbd al-Qāhir al-Jurjānī to critical exuberance was Ibn al-Anbārī's (d. fourth century A.H./ tenth century A.D.) elegiac poem on the crucified vizier Ibn Baqiyyah (d. 367/977) in which the poet "created eloquent magic by reversing the loathsome state of the crucified to its opposite, and then producing wondrous interpretation". Following are the first six lines of Ibn al-Anbārī's poem:

ʿUlūwun fī 'l-ḥayātī wa-fī 'l-mamāti
bi-ḥaqqin anta iḥdā 'l-muʿjizāti
Ka'anna 'n-nāsa ḥawlaka ḥīna qāmū
wufūdu nadāka ayyāma 'ṣ-Ṣilāti
Ka'annaka qā'imun fīhim khaṭīban
wa-kulluhumu qiyāmun li-'ṣ-ʿṢalāti
Madadta yadayka naḥwahumu 'ḥtifā'an
ka-maddihimā ilayhim bi-'l-hibāti
Wa-lammā ḍāqa baṭnu 'l-arḍi ʿan an
yaḍumma ʿulāka min baʿdi 'l-mamāti
Aṣārū 'l-jawwa qabraka wa-'stanābū
ʿani 'l-akfāni thawba 's-sāfiyāti

Elevated in life and in death
You truly are one
of life's miracles
It is as if the people
around you, as you stood,
were seekers of your bounty
on the days of free giving

32. See *Asrār 'l-Balāghah*, Op.Cit., p. 318, and *The Neckveins of Winter*, p. 55.

It is as if you are arisen
among them, a preacher,
and they had risen
for prayer
You stretched out your hands
towards them in welcome
as you had stretched them out
in giving
Since the bowels of the earth
were too strait
to contain your grandeur
after death
they made the sky your grave
and replaced shrouds
with the raiment
of dusty winds.[33]

Medieval "modern" (*muḥdathūn*) poets, practitioners of the New Style (*al-Badīʿ*), resorted to "deception" (*iḥtālū*) in poetic discourse in order to render poetry accessible and credible. This they achieved by employing metaphor and figurative speech and by "creating doubt" (*tashakkuk*) about the point of resemblance in a simile. An example of such doubt creating deception is the following line by Dhū 'l-Rummah (d.117/735):

Fa-yā ẓabyata 'l-waʿsāʾi bayna Jalājilin
wa-bayna 'n-Naqāʾi anti am Ummu Sālimi

O she-gazelle of the sandy ground
between Jalājil and Naqā
Is that you
or Umm Sālim?

The poet created doubt by concealing the identity of both, the gazelle and Umm Sālim, thereby enhancing the appeal of the comparison. Another persuasive creation of doubt is Jarīr's (d.110/728) line:

Fa-innaka law raʾayta ʿabīda Taymin
wa-Tayman qulta ayyahumu 'l-ʿabīdu

---

33. *Asrār 'l-Balāghah*, pp. 321-322, and my article "Death Transformed: A Counter Reading of Crucifixion" in the *Journal of Arabic Literature*, Vol. XXI, Part 1, March 1990, E.J.Brill (Leiden), pp.1-13.

If you had seen
the slaves of Taym
or the Taymis themselves
you would have asked
Who were the slaves?

If Jarīr had said "their slaves" or "the slaves are better than they, the masters," his statement would not have been "perceived as truthful." Instead, the poet resorted to deception (*iḥtāla*) in approximating (*taqrīb*) the comparison, because such comparison possesses "subtlety (*laṭāfah*) that affects a good impression upon the hearts and induces acceptance of the line as truthful."[34]

An additional function of poetic deception and creation of doubt was presented by the later critic Ḥāzim al-Qarṭājannī (d. 684/1285). "What is intended of poetry is deception (*iḥtiyāl*) in stimulating (*taḥrīk*) [a reaction] by the mind to the requisites of discourse, by presenting discourse in an acceptable form to the mind. This is achieved through excellent mimesis and phraseology, and in some instances through truthfulness and commonness."[35] The goal of poetry, in al-Qarṭājannī's scheme, is to stimulate the psyche and to evoke a reaction, favorable or otherwise; the means is deception (*iḥtiyāl*) and falsification (*tamwīh*, misrepresentation; confusion), and the guise is excellent form and imitation.

ʿAbd 'l-Qāhir al-Jurjānī postulated that "poetry can be judged by the images it creates, the innovations it formulates, and the meanings (*maʿānī*, ideas; themes) it instils in the mind."[36] Truthfulness and untruthfulness are attributes of meanings and reside in them. Meanings are of two types: intellectual (*ʿaqlī*, "factual") and imaginative (*takhyīlī*, "poetic"). Intellectual meanings are truthful, accurate, and verifiable. Moreover, they occur within the boundaries of reason, require no metaphoric expression or imaginative recreation, and are readily realized and appreciated.

Conversely, imaginative meanings, untruthful and nonfactual, reside in a supraintellectual realm, that of the imagination.[37] Furthermore, untruthfulness allows the poet "to invent copiously and to display repeatedly the images he has created." Al-Jurjānī proceeded to state that the poet's repertoire of meanings is profuse, unceasing, immeasurable, and inexhaustible. The truthful poet, in contrast, is poetically "fettered" and his creative capabilities are somewhat restricted. "Common meanings and well known images" are the utmost the truthful poet can offer his listeners. His poetic meanings, though perhaps "sublime" (*sharīf*), are like "jewels that can be preserved but are not expected to multiply, or solid substances that neither grow nor expand nor yield any benefit, or like a beautiful but barren woman, or like a luxuriant but unfruitful tree."[38]

34. See Ibn Rashīq, *al-ʿUmdah*, Vol. 2, pp. 53-54, and *The Alchemy of Glory*, pp. 70- 71.

35. See *Minhāj 'l-Bulaghā'*, p. 294, and *The Alchemy of Glory*, p. 117.

36. See *Asrār 'l-Balāghah*, p. 317, and *The Neckveins of Winter*, p. 64.

37. See *Asrār 'l-Balāghah*, pp. 241-245, and *The Alchemy of Glory*, pp. 87-89.

38. See *Asrār 'l-Balāghah*, pp. 250-251, and *The Alchemy of Glory*, pp. 94.

On the other hand, imagination, the provenance and repository of imaginative meanings, "is a deception (*khidāʿ*) of the mind and a form of embellishment (*tazwīq*)," and is demonstrably quite distant from the truth, according to al-Jurjānī. Although imagination is deception, it is not absolute untruthfulness or lying. The "imaginative" poet is primarily a deceiver, but is not a liar. It is absurd, al-Jurjānī warned, to depict the untruthful poet as one who "demonstrates the existence of the nonexistent, and the nonexistence of the nonprivative." More elaborately, "the untruthful poet judges as existent that which does not exist, and as nonexistent (privative) that which is non-privative." In sum, the untruthful poet only judges or assumes the existence of something-- a non-probative act that allows the poet more freedom to imagine and "deceive".[39]

In a similar vein, al-Jurjānī envisioned two types of moderation for poetic truth and untruth. He prescribed an "intermediate course and a medium manner" for expressing factual, truthful meanings if the poet intended to found his judgment on a solid cause or origin. The following two lines by Abū Tammām (d. 231/845) exemplify such a course:

Inna rayba 'z-zamāni yaḥsunu an yuh-
dī 'r-razāyā ilā dhawī 'l-aḥsābi
Fa-li-hādhā yajiffu baʿda 'khḍirārin
qabla rawḍi 'l-wihādi rawḍu 'r-rawābi

It is to the advantage of time
in its vicissitudes
to present misfortunes to the noble-born,
It is for this reason that
luxuriant hill meadows dry up
after verdure
long before the verdant meadows
of the lowlands

As for the expression of untruthful, nonfactual meanings, al-Jurjānī introduced an original literay mode (*namaṭ*), that of "quasifactual imagination" (*takhyīl shabīh bi-'l-ḥaqīqah*). This mode-concept of imaginative expression is "quasifactual" because it is moderate and because "its cause (*ʿillah*) is to be found in its literal meaning." An instance of this type of verisimilar imaginative expression is the following line by Abū Tammām:[40]

Laysa 'l-ḥijābu bi-muqṣin ʿanka lī amalan
inna 's-samāʾa turajjā ḥīna tuḥtajabu

39. See *Asrār 'l-Balāghah*, pp. 252-253, and *The Alchemy of Glory*, pp. 96-97.

40. See *Asrār 'l-Balāghah*, pp. 254-255, and *The Alchemy of Glory*, pp. 97-98.

The curtain will not remove
my hopes of you
Indeed, the skies are beseeched [for rain]
only when they are veiled

The veiling of the sky with clouds is the "reason" for hoping for rain, which was traditionally considered a grace (*niʿmah*) and a bounty descending from the sky in a desert climate. The veil image was an oblique allusion to anticipated generosity from the patron.

Al-Qarṭājannī, on his part, posited an extended role of the imagination: "The mainstay of poetry is the evocation of the imagination (*takhyīl*) and that of rhetoric is persuasion." Poetry is poetry, he further elaborates, not because it is truthful or untruthful, but solely because it is imagination evoking discourse. Moreover, "the truth content (*māddah*) is not important in poetry, but what is significant is the imagination evoking (*takhyīl*) that occurs in such truth content."[41] Moreover, al-Qarṭājannī underscores the necessity of employing untruthfulness in poetry so long as it does not enter the domain of impossibility (*istiḥālah*). He summarizes the general conclusion of late medieval critics: "Untruthfulness can be employed in poetry so long as it does not surpass the realm of the possible or the impossible-but-not-inconceivable (*mumtaniʿ*) to that of the impossible-and-inconceivable (*mustaḥīl*), even though the impression on the psyche of the *mumtaniʿ* is inferior to that of the possible." Al-Qarṭājannī cites the following lines by al-Mutanabbī as an example of such poetic discourse:

Wa-annā 'htadā hādhā 'r-rasūlu bi-arḍihi
wa-mā sakanat mudh sirta fīhā 'l-qasāṭilu
Wa-min ayyī mā'in kāna yasqī jiyādahu
wa-lam taṣfu min mazji 'd-dimā'i 'l-manāhilu

How could this messenger have found
his way through the battlefield
when the dust, since you marched in it,
has not yet settled!
And which springs did he lead his horses to
when none of the watering places
has been cleared of blood

Exaggeration in these two lines is "appropriate and acceptable," al-Qarṭājannī determined, because it is possible to "envision the existence" of an innumerable army and the infinite spillage of blood, even though neither exists in reality.[42]

41. See *Minhāj 'l-Bulaghā'*, pp. 63, 71, 83, and *The Alchemy of Glory*, pp. 103, 113.

42. See *Minhāj 'l-Bulaghā'*, pp. 135-136, and *The Alchemy of Glory*, pp. 115-116.

Medieval Arab critics notwithstanding, Arab poets never composed poetry according to critical standards, nor did they abide by the canonical rules of poetry. They certainly refrained from confining their creativity to the realm of the possible, the only conceivable, or the truthful. Indeed, the most selectable poetry was verses that ushered both intellectual and imaginative meanings and images into the realm of the impossible, inconceivable, untruthful, hyperbolic, metaphorical, and absurd. Such cited verses are included in this anthology.

The present bilingual topical anthology of celebrated classical Arabic hyperbolic verses mostly includes single lines, occasionally two or more lines, and in a few cases short poems, which were selected and characterized by medieval critics as "best" in their subject. The medieval critics interpreted and compared such verses to others on the same subject or theme within the framework of the medieval New Style (*al-Badīʿ*), which was synonymous with the extravagant employment of figures of speech, especially of metaphor and simile, and within the context of the dialectic of poetic truthfulness and untruthfulness.

Excluded from this anthology is aphoristic, gnomic, didactic, homiletic, religious, semi-epic, political and ethical poetry, as well as plain doggerel. The verses compiled here were deemed by medieval critics to be the "best" and "most selectable" of whatever subject or theme; they encompass such genres as description, elegy, panegyric, satire (including invective poetry; lampooning), boasting, love poetry (*ghazal*), wine poems and other genres written between the sixth and the fourteenth century A.D.

I have added a few extra-critical selections in order to augment the samples on a certain rather underrepresented theme or topic. These include a verse from the *Lāmiyyat al-ʿArab* of Zayn 'l-Dīn ʿUmar Ibn 'l-Wardī (d. 749/1348), two verses by Ashjaʿ al-Sulamī (d. 190/805), a short poem by Maysūn bint Baḥdal (d. ca. 80/700), the wife of the Caliph Muʿāwiyah ibn Abī Sufyān (60/680, reigned 41/661) whom he married before he became caliph, and a few lines by an anonymous Bedouin woman poet. Otherwise, the samples were culled from the critics' choice in select medieval ctitical treatises.

The translation is mine save for several lines superbly translated by British scholars, as indicated in the text. I have rendered the translation as faithfully to the original and as accurately reflective of the critics' own comprehension of the verses as possible. Such strict lexical rendition is intended to validate any interpretation of the various meanings of a word or phrase; the ideas and images were left in their pristine state whenever possible, so that they might reflect the distinct literary, cultural invention, as well as the aesthetic sensibility of the Arab poetic mind and of medieval Arabic poetry during that long period of time and over a vast geographic expanse. On the whole, it is an interpretive reading translation of the Arabic, with occasional semantic explication or cultural references to certain themes or images or phrases.

An intriguing conventional poetic practice in medieval Arabic poetry was the employment of the masculine to refer to either sex or occasionally to the feminine exclusively. The primary reason for such usage is the metrical, rhyming, and syntactical convenience and ease of the masculine. The masculine scans better syntactically and prosodically, and it is less cumbersome to employ the shorter and more versatile masculine form than the feminine suffix, especially in the second and third feminine plural. Other considerartions, such as concealing the identity of the beloved for the sake of propriety, or consciously endeavoring to maintain secrecy for both putative lovers, have contributed to the pervasiveness of the practice. It is not always uncertain that the subject of description is a woman. As well, some poets did write love poetry (*ghazal*) about young lads (*ghazal al-ghilmān*) and women alike. In order to avert inappropriate speculation and to honor the prevailing usage of the masculine in reference to a woman (especially in love poetry), I have maintained the original gender usage, whether masculine or feminine, in the selected verses.

The death dates of poets, critics and others in the introduction and in the text of the anthology are accepted approximations. The real dates cannot be accurately determined, largely because of the yearly eleven-day difference between the Muslim and Christian calendars, as well as the traditionally inaccurate reporting of dates in medieval Arabic. The death dates of a number of poets were not available; many cited lines were composed by anonymous poets, and occasionally the same line or lines were attributed to more than one poet.

On Generosity

ما قالَ لا قَطُّ إلاَّ في تَشَهُّدِه
لَوْلا التَّشَهُّدُ كانَتْ لاؤهُ نَعَم
الفرزدق

He only said “no”
when professing the *shahādah*
Had it not been
for the *shahādah*,
his ‘no’ would
have been “yes”

al-Farazdaq (d.110/728)

“Shahādah,” the confessional creed or profession of faith, is the Muslim doctrinal formula: “There is no deity but God and Muḥammad is His messenger.” It is the first of the five fundamental tenets, or pillars, of Islam. Al-Farazdaq’s line is described by medieval Arab literary commentators as the best verse ever composed on generosity.

أَثْمَرَتْ أَغْصانُ راحَتِه
لِجُناةِ الحُسْنِ عُنَّابا
إبن المعتزّ

The branches of his palm
have borne fruit,
jujube,
for those who reap
his beneficence

Ibn al-Muʿtazz (d. 296/908)

وعَجِبْتُ مِنْ أَرْضٍ سَحابُ أَكَفِّهِمْ
مِنْ فَوْقِها وَصُخُورُها لا تُورِقُ
المتنبِّي

I marvel at a land
whose rocks do not sprout
green leaves
when the rain clouds
of their hands
pour forth
on it

al-Mutanabbī (d. 354/965)

In the medieval Arabic hierarchy of cultural values, hands are compared to rain-bearing clouds, the utmost form of generosity in a desert society.

لَو كانَ يَقْعُدُ فَوْقَ الشَّمْسِ مِنْ كَرَمٍ
قَوْمٌ بِأَحْسابِهِمْ أَوْ مَجْدِهِمْ قَعَدوا
زُهَير بن أبي سُلمى

Were it possible for a people
to sit atop the sun,
for their generosity,
glory and noble descent,
they are the ones
who would do so

Zuhayr ibn Abī Sulmā (d. 609 A.D.)

تَراهُ إذا ما جِئْتَهُ مُتَهَلِّلاً
كأَنَّكَ مُعْطِيهِ الّذي أَنْتَ سائِلُهْ
زُهَير بن أَبي سُلمى

You will find him jubilant
when you come to see him
as if you are giving him
what you have come
to ask for

Zuhayr ibn Abī Sulmā (d. ca. 609 A.D.)

تَعَوَّدَ بَسْطَ الكَفِّ حَتَّى لَو اَنَّهُ
ثَناها لِقَبْضٍ لَمْ تُطِعْهُ أَنامِلُهْ
وَلَو لَمْ يَكُنْ في كَفِّهِ غَيْرُ نَفْسِه
لَجادَ بِها، فَلْيَتَّقِ اللهَ سائِلُهْ
أَبو تمَّام

He is so wont
to extend his hand
in giving
that, were he to clench his hand,
his fingers would not obey him,
And if he had nothing but his soul
in his hand*
he would give it away
May those who seek his generosity
have fear of God

Abū Tammām (d. 231/845)

* An open hand is a symbol of generosity.

لَو لَمْ تُفَتِّ مُسِنَّ المَجْدِ مُذْ زَمَنٍ
بِالجُودِ والبَأْسِ كانَ الجُودُ قَدْ خَرِفا
أبو تمَّام

Had you not,
in long time past,
with boldness and generosity,
rendered old glory youthful,
generosity would have
become senile

Abū Tammām (d. 231/ 845)

لَيْسَ الحِجابُ بِمُقْصٍ عَنْكَ لي أَمَلاً
إنَّ السَّماءَ تُرَجَّى حينَ تُحْتَجَبُ
أبو تمَّام

The veil* will not distance
my hope [of generosity] from you
Verily, the sky is beseeched for rain
only when it is veiled**

Abū Tammām (d. 231/845)

* The veil refers to a curtain or screen that was sometimes used to separate a person of high rank or a woman from a poet or one seeking an audience.
** A "veiled" sky is cloudy.

إنَّ السَّحابَ لَتَسْتَحْيي إذا نَظَرَتْ
إلى نداكَ فقاسَتْهُ بِما فيها
أبو نُواس

Rain clouds would be embarrassed
to look at your generosity
and compare it
to their own

Abū Nuwās (d. 198/813)

لا تُنْكِري عَطَلَ الكَريم مِنَ الغنى
فالسَّيْلُ حَرْبٌ لِلْمَكانِ العالي
أبو تمَّام

Do not find fault
with a generous man
if he is destitute of wealth,
for floodwater is at odds
with high peaks

Abū Tammām (d. 231/ 845)

وَمَنْ ذا يَلُومُ البَحْرَ إنْ باتَ زاخِراً
يَفيضُ وصَوْبَ المُزْنِ إنْ راحَ يَهْطُلُ
البحتري

Whoever would blame the brim-full sea
if it overflowed
Or rain clouds
if they suddenly
poured down

al-Buḥturī (d. 284/897)

وَما ثَناكَ كَلامُ النَّاسِ عَنْ كَرَمٍ
وَمَنْ يَسُدُّ طَريقَ العارِضِ الهَطِلِ
المتنبِّي

People's talk has not checked
your generosity
Whosoever could block
the course
of sudden heavy rain?

al-Mutanabbī (d. 354/965)

تَراهُ إذا ما أَبْصَرَ الضَّيْفَ كَلْبُهُ
يُكَلِّمُهُ مِنْ حُبِّهِ وَهْوَ أَعْجَمُ
ابن حمرة

No sooner does his dog
see a guest
than it will,
out of love and hospitality,
talk to him,
even though the dog
is speechless

Ibn Ḥamrah (n.d.)

هُوَ البَحْرُ مِنْ أيِّ النَّواحي أَتَيْتَهُ
فَلُجَّتُهُ الْمَعْروفُ والْجُودُ ساحِلُهْ
أَبو تَمَّام

He is the sea
whencesoever you come to him
Beneficence is his depth
and liberality his shore

Abū Tammām (d. 231/845)

A very generous man is compared to the sea.

On Life

إذا كُنْتَ عِزْهاةً عَنِ اللَّهْوِ والصِّبا
فَكُنْ حَجَراً مِنْ يابِسِ الصَّخْرِ جَلْمَدا
فَما العَيْشُ إلاَّ ما تُحِبُّ وَتَشْتَهي
وَإنْ لامَ فيهِ ذُو الشِّنانِ وَفَنَّدا
الأَحْوَص

If you abstain from pleasure
and youthful passion
you might as well be
a large, hard, desiccated rock
Life is naught
but what you love and desire
no matter how much the envious
scold and conspire

al-Aḥwaṣ (d. 105/723)

يَهْوى البَقاءَ رَهْبَةَ الفَناءِ
وَإنَّما يَفْنى مِنَ البَقاءِ
عبد الصَّمَد بن المُعَذَّل

He loves long life
for fear of perdition
But he perishes
because of long life

ʿAbd al-Ṣamad ibn al-Muʿadhdhal (n.d.)

وَلَعَلَّ ما تَخْشاهُ لَيْسَ بِكائِنٍ
وَلَعَلَّ ما تَرْجُوهُ سَوْفَ يَكُونُ
وَلَعَلَّ ما هَوَّنْتَ لَيْسَ بِهَيِّنٍ
وَلَعَلَّ ما شَدَّدْتَ سَوْفَ يَهُونُ
أَبو العَتَاهِية

Perhaps what you fear
does not exist
Perhaps what you wish
will come to be
Perhaps what you deem easy
is not so easy
And perhaps what you think hard
will be easy

Abū 'l-ʿAtāhiyah (d. 209/824 or -5)

وَأَعْمارُنا أَبْياتُ شِعْرٍ كَأَنَّما
أَواخِرُها لِلْمُنْشِدِينَ قَوافِ
المَعَرِّي

Our lives are naught
but lines that scan
Then comes the rhyme
so ends the man

Abū 'l-ʿAlā' al-Maʿarrī (d. 449/1057)
British translation

إِنَّ أَعْمارَنا كَآيٍ أُبِينَتْ
وَالْمَنايا لَهُنَّ مِثْلُ الفَواصِل
المَعَرِّي

Our life is but
a phrase, a breath
Then comes full-stop
and that's our death

Abū 'l-ʿAlāʾ al-Maʿarrī (d. 449/1057)
British translation

إنَّما نِعْمةُ قَوْمٍ مُتْعَةٌ
وَحَياةُ المَرْءِ ثَوْبٌ مُسْتَعارْ
الأَفْوَه الأَودي

Verily, the boon of a people
is fleeting pleasure
and a man's life
is but a borrowed garment

al-Afwah al-Awdī (d. 570 A.D.)

وَإِذا الشَّيْخُ قالَ: أُفٍّ، فَما مَلَّ
حَياةً وَإِنَّما الضَّعْفَ مَلاَّ
المتنبِّي

When an old man cries "ugh"!
He is not tired of life
but only tired
of feebleness

al-Mutanabbī (d. 354/965)

Translated by R. J. Nicholson in *A Literary History of the Arabs*, p. 312)

وَما عِشْتُ حَتَّى اليَوْمَ إلاَّ لأنَّني
خَفيتُ وَلَمْ يَدْرِ الحِمامُ مَكاني
البَهاء زُهَيْر

I am alive today
only because I hid myself
from death
and death knows not
where to find me

al-Bahā' Zuhayr (d. 657/1258)

On Time and Days

تَغَطَّيْتُ مِنْ دَهْرِي بِظِلِّ جَناحِه
فَعَيْنِي تَرى دَهْرِي وَلَيْسَ يَرانِي
فَلَوْ تُسْأَلُ الأَيَّامُ ما ٱسْمِي ما دَرَتْ
وَأَيْنَ مَكانِي ما عَرَفْنَ مَكانِي
أَبو نُواس

I shielded myself from time*
with the shadow
of its wings
So my eyes see time
but time sees me not
If the days were asked
about my name
they would not know it
and about my abode
they would not know
where I am

Abū Nuwās (d. 198/814)

Time (*dahr, zamān, zaman*) in the Arab mind signifies days, fate, eternity, death, long time or long life, good or bad life. When used in a construct phrase, time means vicissitudes or blows of fate, misfortunes, trials and tribulations, adversities etc. "Days", which also means life, is used interchangeably with "time", especially when made necessary by the exigencies of meter and/or rhyme. *"fa-law tus'alu 'l-ayyāmu"* can also be read as *"fa-law tas'ali 'l-ayyāma"*: Were you to ask the days.

وَما كُنْتُ إلاَّ كَالزَّمانِ إذا صَحا
صَحَوْتُ، وَإنْ ماقَ الزَّمانُ أَمُوقُ
بشَّار بن بُرد

I am but like time–
If it is sober and awake
I am sober and awake,
And if it acts foolishly*
I do the same

Bashshār ibn Burd (d. 167/784)

"Māqa" (to act foolishly) also means to perish.

تَرُوحُ عَلَيْنا كُلَّ يَوْمٍ وَتَغْتَدي
خُطُوبٌ يَكادُ الدَّهْرُ مِنْهُنَّ يُصْرَعُ
أبو تمَّام

Calamities visit us
morning and evening,
so hard and so often,
that even time
is almost felled
by them

Abū Tammām (d. 231/845)

The rhyme word *"yuṣraʿu"* (felled by them) can also mean: rendered epileptic. Thus, time is felled or rendered epileptic by its own calamities.

وَلَيَّنَ لي دَهْري بإِتْباعِ جُودِهِ
فَكِدْتُ لِلِينِ الدَّهْرِ أَنْ أَعْقِدَ الدَّهْرا
والِد الخَثْعَمِي

His generosity has made my time
so supple and easy
that I can almost tie such time*
into a knot.

Wālid al-Khathʿamī (n.d.)

* The first word "time" means life; the second one signifies time that can be measured in passing, as days, years etc.

أَتى الزَّمانَ بَنُوهُ في شَبيبَتِه
فَسَرَّهُمْ وَأَتَيْناهُ عَلى الهَرَمِ
المتنبِّي

Ancient people came to life
when time was young and fresh
and it made them happy
But alas! we have come to life
when time is old
and decrepit

al-Mutanabbī (d. 354/965)

يا دَهْرُ قَوِّمْ مِنْ أَخْدَعَيْكَ فَقَدْ
أَضْجَجْتَ هَذا الأَنامَ مِنْ خُرُقِكْ
أبو تمَّام

O time!
Straighten your neckveins
for you have drowned mankind
with your clamorous clumsiness

Abū Tammām (d. 231/845)

تَحَمَّلْتُ ما لَوْ حُمِّلَ الدَّهْرُ شَطْرَهُ
لَفَكَّرَ دَهْراً أَيُّ عِبْأَيْهِ أَثْقَلُ
أَبو تمَّام

If time were to endure
half of what I have endured
It would have to ponder long
about which of its two burdens
was heavier

Abū Tammām (d. 231/845)

وَكَمْ أَحْرَزَتْ مِنْكُمْ عَلى قُبْحِ قَدِّها
صُرُوفُ الرَّدى مِنْ مُرْهَفٍ حَسَنِ القَدِّ
أَبو تمَّام

How many of your men,
slender and of fine physique,
have the ravages of time,
despite their turpitude,
carefully preserved

Abū Tammām (d. 231/845)

أَنْزَلَتْهُ الأَيَّامُ عَنْ ظَهْرِها مِنْ
بَعْدِ إِثْبَاتِ رِجْلِهِ في الرِّكابِ
أَبو تمَّام في رثاء فتىً

The days have dismounted him
from their backs
after he had steadied his feet
in their stirrups

Abū Tammām (d. 231/845)

كَأَنَّني حِينَ جَرَّدْتُ الرَّجاءَ لَهُ
عَضْبًا صَبَبْتُ بِهِ ماءً عَلى الزَّمَنِ
أبو تمَّام

It was as though I poured water
on time
when I unsheathed hope,
a sharp sword,
to protect him
against time

Abū Tammām (d.231/845))

ضَحِكْنا وَكانَ الضَّحْكُ مِنَّا سَفاهةً
وَحُقَّ لِسُكَّانِ البَسيطةِ أَنْ يَبْكُوا
تُحَطِّمُنا الأَيَّامُ حَتَّى كَأَنَّنا
زُجاجٌ وَلَكِنْ لا يُعادُ لَهُ سَبْكُ
أبو العلاء المَعَرِّي

We laugh, but inept is our laughter;
We should weep and weep sore,
Who are shattered like glass,
and thereafter,
Re-moulded no more

Abū 'l-ʿAlā' al-Maʿarrī (d. 449/1057)

Translated by R. A. Nicholson in *A Literary History of the Arabs*, p. 316.

عَجِبْتُ لِسَعْيِ الدَّهْرِ بَيْنِي وَبَيْنَها
فَلَمَّا ٱنْقَضى ما بَيْنَنا سَكَنَ الدَّهْرُ
أبو صَخْرِ الهُذَلِيّ

I marvel at time,
how swiftly it sped
between me and her
But when all was finished
between us
time came to a standstill

Abū Ṣakhr al-Hudhalī (2nd half of seventh century A.D.)

وَإنِّي وَإنْ كُنْتُ الأَخِيرَ زَمانُهُ
لآتٍ بِما لَمْ تَسْتَطِعْهُ الأَوائِلُ
أبو العلاء المَعَرِّي

And I, albeit I come in Time's late hour,
Achieve what lay not
in the ancients' power

Abū 'l-ʿAlā' al-Maʿarrī (d. 449/1057)

Translated by R. A. Nicholson in *Studies in Islamic Poetry*, p. 49.

هَلِ الدَّهْرُ إلاَّ لَيْلَةٌ وَنَهارُها
وَإلاَّ طُلُوعُ الشَّمْسِ ثُمَّ غِيابُها
لأَحدهم

Is Time aught but night
and its following day
And aught but the rising
of the sun
and then its
setting

Anonymous

Translated by W. Wright in *A Grammar of the Arabic Language*, p. 339.

On Gray Hair and Youth

أَلشَّيْبُ كُرْهٌ وَكُرْهٌ أَنْ يُفارِقَني
أَعْجِبْ بِشَيْءٍ عَلى البَغْضاءِ مَوْدُودِ
ابن المُعْتَزّ

Gray hair is loathsome
but loathsome also
is its departure
Marvel at a thing,
though being loathed,
is so loved
and desired

Ibn al-Muʿtazz (d. 296/908)

وَبَياضُ البازِيِّ أَصْدَقُ حُسْنًا
إِنْ تَأَمَّلْتَ مِنْ سَوادِ الغُرابِ
البحتري

The whiteness of the hawk
is truly more beautiful,
if you ponder it,
than the blackness
of the crow

al-Buḥturī (d. 284/897)

وَالصَّارِمُ المَصْقُولُ أَحْسَنُ حالَةً
يَوْمَ الوَغى مِنْ صارِمٍ لَمْ يُصْقَلِ
لأحدهم

A burnished sword*
is more effective
in battle
than an unburnished one

Anonymous

A burnished sword denotes gray hair, and along with it prudence and wisdom.

قَدْ يَشِيبُ الفَتى وَلَيْسَ عَجِيبًا
أَنْ يُرى النَّوْرُ في القَضِيبِ الرَّطِيبِ
ابن الرُّومي

A young man may gray quickly–
Marvel not,
for white blossoms
can be seen
on a young and tender branch

Ibn al-Rūmī (d. 283/896)

وَالشَّيْبُ يَنْهَضُ في الشَّباب كَأَنَّهُ
لَيْلٌ يَصِيحُ بِجانِبَيْهِ نَهارُ
الفَرَزْدَق

Gray hair rises in youth
as if it were a night
flanked by a bawling day

al-Farazdaq (d. 110/728)

لا تَعْجَبي يا سَلْمُ مِنْ رَجُلٍ
ضَحِكَ المَشِيبُ بِرأْسِهِ فَبَكى
دِعْبِل الخزاعي

Marvel not, O Salmā, at a man
who wept
when gray hair grinned
on his head

Diʿbil al-Khuzāʿī (d. 246/860)

ضَيْفٌ أَلَمَّ بِرأْسِي غَيْرَ مُحْتَشِم
أَلسَّيْفُ أَحْسَنُ فِعْلاً مِنْهُ بِاللِّمَمِ
إِبْعِدْ بَعِدْتَ بَيَاضًا لا بَيَاضَ لَهُ
لأَنْتَ أَسْوَدُ في عَيْنِي مِنَ الظُّلَمِ
بِحُبِّ قاتِلَتي وَالشَّيْبُ تَغْذِيَتي
هَوايَ طِفْلاً وَشَيْبي بالِغَ الحُلُمِ
المتنبِّي

A shameless guest
alighted on my head
I would rather take the stroke
of a sword
Perish, O you non-white whiteness!
To me, you are more black
than all darkness
Love nourished me
when I was a child
and nourished my gray hair
when I reached puberty

al-Mutanabbī (d. 354/956)

Al-Mutanabbī was in love when he was young and had gray hair when he reached puberty.

فَإِنْ تَسْأَلُونِي بِالنِّساءِ فَإِنَّني
بَصيرٌ بِأَدْواءِ النِّساءِ طَبيبُ
إِذا شابَ شَعْرُ المَرْءِ أَوْ قَلَّ مالُهُ
فَلَيْسَ لَهُ في وُدِّهِنَّ نَصيبُ
يُرِدْنَ ثَراءَ المالِ حَيْثُ وَجَدْنَهُ
وَشَرْخُ الشَّبابِ عِنْدَهُنَّ عَجيبُ
عَلْقَمة بن عَبْدَة

Women's ills I'm wise to diagnose:
If a lover ages
or his money goes,
So ends their love.
It's money they adore
Wher e'er it be:
In youth and strength alone
they greatness see

ʿAlqamah ibn ʿAbdah (d. 598 A.D.)

British translation.

إِنَّ شَرْخَ الشَّبابِ وَالشَّعَرَ الأَسْوَدَ
ما لَمْ يُعاصَ كانَ جُنُونَا
حَسَّان بن ثابت

Prime of youth
and black hair
are madness
so long as they are not
disobeyed

Ḥassān ibn Thābit (d. 54/674)

أَرادَ الشَّيْبُ مِنِّي خَتْلَ نَفْسِي
لأَنْسَى ذِكْرَ رَبَّاتِ الحِجالِ
إِذا اخْتَصَمَ الصِّبا والشَّيْبُ عِنْدي
فَأَفْلَجْتُ الشَّبابَ فَلا أُبالي
أَبو صَخْرٍ الهُذَلِي

Gray hair wanted me
to deceive myself
so I could forget the memory
of young ladies
Were my youth and gray hair
to quarrel
and I let youth win
I surely would not care

Abū Ṣakhr al-Hudhalī (d. 2nd half of 7th century A.D.)

كَفاكَ بِالشَّيْبِ ذَنْبًا عِنْدَ غانِيَةٍ
وَبِالشَّبابِ شَفِيعًا أَيُّها الرَّجُلُ
أبو حازم الباهِلِيّ

Suffice it to you, O man,
that gray hair is an offense
to a beautiful belle
and that youth
is an intercessor with her

Abū Ḥāzim al-Bāhilī (n.d.)

ما كُنْتُ أُوفِي شَبابي كُنْهَ غِرَّتِه
حَتَّى ٱنْقَضى فَإِذا الدُّنْيا لَهُ تَبَعُ
النَّمرِي

I had hardly fulfilled
the utmost vanity

of my youth
before it came to an end
and lo!
Life followed

al-Namirī (n.d.)

عَرِيْتُ من الشَّبابِ وكان غَضًّا
كما يَعْرَى من الورَق القضيبُ
ألا ليتَ الشَّبابَ يَعُودُ يومًا
فأُخبِرَهُ بِما صَنَعَ المَشِيبُ
أبو العتاهية

I was stripped of youth
when it was fresh and tender
as a branch is stripped
of its leaves
Oh, how I wish that youth
would return!
so I could tell it
what gray hair has wrought

Abū 'l-ʿAtāhiyah (d. 210/825)

وَفَقْدُ الشَّبابِ الْمَوْتُ يُوجَدُ طَعْمُهُ
صُراحًا وطَعْمُ الْمَوْتِ بِالْمَوْتِ يُفْقَدُ
ابن الرومي

Loss of youth is death
whose taste is pure,
whereas the taste of death
is lost by death

Ibn al-Rūmī, ʿAlī ibn al-ʿAbbās (d. 896/283)

رَمَتْني وَسِتْرُ اللهِ بَيْني وَبَيْنَها
عَشِيَّةَ آرامِ الْكِناسِ رَميمُ
أَلا رُبَّ يَوْمٍ لَوْ رَمَتْني رَمَيْتُها
وَلَكِنَّ عَهْدي بِالنِّضالِ قَديمُ
أبو حيَّة النُّميري

Ramīm cast her eyes upon me
that evening at Ārām 'l-Kinās
when grayness* had come
between us
Oh for the days,
when if she had cast her eyes
upon me,
I would have returned her glance
But alas! My days
of amatory struggle
are long past

Abū Ḥayyah al-Numayrī (d. 183/799)

The Arabic for "grayness" *"sitru 'l-lāh"* was given different meanings by medieval literary historians/critics (*e.g.* al-Mubarrad (d. 285 or 286/898 or 899), including: fear of God; modesty; veiled intentions, veil, curtain, screen, shame, Islam, forbidden pleasures. I opted for the meaning: grayness or old age, because the poet was lamenting the loss of youth when it was most needed.

قالَتْ: كَبِرْتَ وشِبْتَ، قُلْتُ لها:
هذا غُبارُ وَقائعِ الدَّهْرِ
إبن المعتزّ

She said: you have grown old
and your hair has become gray
I said to her:
This is the dust
of the battles
of days

Ibn al-Muʿtazz (d. 296/908)

تَعيبُ الغانياتُ عَلَيَّ شَيْبي
ومَنْ لي أن أُمتَّعَ بالمَشيبِ
البُحْتُري

Beautiful women shame me
for my gray hair
How can I ever enjoy
old age?

Al-Buḥturī (d. 284/897)

ولا يُرَوِّعْكَ إيماضُ القَتيرِ بِهِ
فَإِنَّ ذاكَ ٱبْتِسامُ الرأْيِ وَالأدَبِ
أبو تمَّام

Do not be frightened
by the first appearance
of faintly shining
hoariness
It is but the smiling
of wisdom
and knowledge

Abū Tammām (d. 231/845)

صَحا الْقَلْبُ عَنْ سَلْمى وَأَقْصَرَ باطِلُهْ
وَعُرِّيَ أَفْراسُ الصِّبا وَرَواحِلُهْ
زُهَير بن أبي سُلمى

My heart awoke from Salmā's love
when its vanity reached
its sunset
And the horses and camels
of youth
have indeed been
unsaddled

Zuhayr ibn Abī Sulmā (d. 13/627)

أُحِبُّ الشَّيْبَ لَمَّا قِيلَ ضَيْفٌ
كَحُبِّي لِلضُّيُوفِ النَّازِلِينا
دِعْبِل

I loved gray hair
when they said:
it was a guest,
just as I love guests
who are here to stay

Diʿbil al-Khuzāʿī (d. 246/860)

On The Length of a Lover's Night

أَبُدِّلَ اللَّيْلُ لا تَسْري كَواكِبُهُ
أَمْ طالَ حَتَّى حَسِبْتُ النَّجْمَ حَيْرانا
جرير

Has the night changed
and its stars not moved
Or has it become so long
that methinks the stars
are utterly confused ?

Jarīr (d.110/728)

والليلُ من وَجْدي إذا أَمْهَلْتُهُ
يَعْصى ويَسْتَعْصي الغَرامُ إذا صَبا
لأَحدهم

The night,
because of my ardent love,
rebels if I try
to slow it down
and love would be restrained
if the night were to become young

Anonymous

وَلَيْلٍ كَمَوْجِ البَحْرِ أَرْخَى سُدُولَهُ
عَلَيَّ بِأَنْوَاعِ الهُمُومِ لِيَبْتَلِي
فَقُلْتُ لَهُ لَمّا تَمَطَّى بِصُلْبِهِ
وَأَرْدَفَ أَعْجَازاً وَنَاءَ بِكَلْكَلِ
أَلا أَيُّها اللّيْلُ الطَّوِيلُ أَلا ٱنْجَلِ
بِصُبْحٍ وَمَا الإصْباحُ مِنْكَ بِأَمْثَلِ
فَيا لَكَ مِنْ لَيْلٍ كَأَنَّ نُجُومَهُ
بِأَمْراسِ كَتَّانٍ إلى صُمِّ جَنْدَلِ
وفي بعض المراجع:
فَيا لَكَ مِنْ لَيْلٍ كَأَنَّ نُجُومَهُ
بِكُلِّ مَغارِ الفَتْلِ شُدَّتْ بِيَذْبُلِ
امرؤ القيس

Many a night,
dark as the waves of the sea,
has let down its curtains upon me
to try me
And I said to the night,
when it stretched its lazy loins
followed by its fat buttocks
and heaved off its heavy breast,
Well now, you tedious long night,
won't you clear yourself off
and let dawn shine?
Yet dawn, when it comes, is in no way
better than you
Oh, what a night of nights you are!
It's as though the stars
were tied to the Mount of Yadhbul
with infinite hempen ropes;*

Imru' al-Qays (d. ca. 545 A.D.)

* Another version of the last line reads as: "it is as though the Pleiades/ in their stable/ were firmly hung by stout flax cables/ to craggy slabs of granite".
Translated by A. J. Arberry in The Seven Odes, p. 64.

كِليني لِهَمٍّ، يا أُمَيْمَةَ، ناصِبِ
وَلَيْلٍ أُقاسيهِ بَطِيءِ الكَواكِبِ
تَطاوَلَ حَتَّى قُلْتُ لَيْسَ بِمُنْقَضٍ
وَلَيْسَ الّذي يَرْعَى النُّجُومَ بِآيِبِ
بِصَدْرٍ أَراحَ اللَّيْلُ عازِبَ هَمِّه
تَضاعَفَ فيهِ الحُزْنُ مِنْ كُلِّ جانِبِ
النابغة الذبياني

O Umaymah! Let me endure
exhausting grief
and the slow-moving stars
of night
The night stretched so long
that I thought it would never end
and those who herd the stars
would never go home
All of that I endured
with a heart
unto which the night
brought grief from
remote pastures
and in which all-exhaustive grief
has multiplied

al-Nābighah al-Dhubyānī (d. ca. 604 A.D.)

فَنامَ لَيْلي وَتَجَلَّى هَمِّي
رؤبة بن العجَّاج

My night fell asleep
and my cares vanished

Ru'bah ibn al-ʿAjjāj (d. 145/ 762)

رَقَدْتَ ولَمْ تَرْثِ لِلسَّاهِرِ
ولَيْلُ المُحِبِّ بِلا آخِرِ
خالد الكاتب

You have slept with no pity
for the wakeful lover
Indeed, the night of lovers
has no end

Khālid al-Kātib (d. 262/ 875)

لِخَدَّيْكَ مِنْ كَفَّيْكَ في كُلِّ لَيْلَةٍ
إلى أَنْ تَرَى ضَوْءَ الصَّباحِ وِسادُ
تَبيتُ تُراعي اللَّيْلَ تَرْجُو نَفادَهُ
ولَيْسَ لِلَيْلِ العاشِقينَ نَفادُ
بشَّار بن بُرْد

Your hands pillow your cheeks
every night
until you see dawn's light
You stay awake watching the night
hoping it will exhaust itself
But alas! There is no end
to lovers' night

Bashshār ibn Burd (d. 167/ 783)

On Love Induced Emaciation

ولَو أَنَّ ما أَبْقَيْتِ مِنِّي مُعَلَّقٌ
بِعُودِ ثَمامٍ ما تَأَوَّدَ عُودُها
يُنْسَب إلى الأعْشى

If what you have left of me
were hung from a stalk
of panic grass
the stalk would not bend

Attributed to al-Aʿshā (d. 7/629)

أُسَرُّ إِذا نَحُلْتُ وَذابَ جِسْمي
لَعَلَّ الرِّيحَ تَسْفي بي إِلَيْهِ
لأحدهم

I would rejoice
if I became emaciated
and my body pined away
Perhaps then
the wind would blow me
towards him

Anonymous

ذابَ فَلَوْ زُجَّ بِجُسْمانِهِ
في ناظِرِ الوَسْنانِ لَمْ يَنْتَبِهْ
لأحدهم

He has so pined away,
Were his body to be pressed
into the eye
of a sleeping person,
he would not awaken

Anonymous

وَلَوْ قَلَمٌ أُلْقيتُ في شِقِّ رأْسِه
مِنَ السُّقْمِ ما غَيَّرْتُ في خَطِّ كاتِبِ
المتنبِّي

Were I to be placed
on the split tip
of a quill
I would not,
for my love-sickness,
change the penmanship
of a scribe

al-Mutanabbī (d. 354/965)

كَفى بِجِسْمي نُحولاً أَنَّني رَجُلٌ
لَوْلا مُخاطَبَتي إيّاكَ لَمْ تَرَني
المتنبِّي

Suffice it to you
that I am
so love-emaciated
that, had I not been talking
to you,
you would not have seen me

al-Mutanabbī (d. 354/965)

أَلا إنَّما غادَرْتِ يا أُمَّ مالك
صَدًى أَيْنَما تَذْهَبْ بِهِ الرِّيحُ يَذْهَبِ
لأحدهم

O Umm Mālik!
You have left behind
but an echo
that blows with the wind
wherever it blows

Anonymous

ذُبْتُ مِنَ الشَّوْقِ، فَلَوْ زُجَّ بي
في مُقْلَةِ النَّائِمِ لَمْ يَنْتَبِهْ
وَكانَ لي فيما مَضى خاتَمٌ
فَالْلآنَ لَوْ شِئْتُ تَمَنْطَقْتُ بِهْ
نَصْر الخُبْزَرْزي (أو الخبزأرزي)

I have pined away with longing,
Were I to be squeezed
into the eye of a sleeper
he would not awaken
I once had a ring,
Were I now to gird myself
with it
I could surely do it

Naṣr al-Khubzarzī (or al-Khubz 'aruzzī) (d. 328/ 939)

لَمَّا بَلِيتُ مِنَ الهَوى
خِفْتُ العُيونَ مِنْ أنْ تَراني
لَوْلا كَلامي ما ٱهْتَدَتْ
عَيْنُ الجَليسِ إلى مَكاني
محمَّد بن يحيى

As I wasted away for love
I was afraid
that eyes could no longer see me
Had I not been talking
My companions would not have found
where I was

Muḥammad ibn Yaḥyā (n.d.)

بَيْنَ ثِيابي جَسَدٌ ناحِلٌ
لَوْ هَبَّتِ الرِّيحُ بِهِ طاحا
بشَّار بن بُرْد

A gaunt body lives
in my clothes,
Were the wind
to blow on it
it would be swept away

Bashshār ibn Burd (d. 167/728)

إنَّ في بُرْدَيَّ جِسْمًا ناحِلاً
لَوْ تَوَكَّأْتِ عَلَيْهِ لانْهَدَمْ
بشَّار بن بُرْد

My clothes house a lean body,
Were you to lean on it
It would surely
collapse

Bashshār ibn Burd (d. 167/728)

فاسْتَبْقِ ما أَبْقَيْتِ لي فَلَعَلَّني
يَوْمًا أَقيكِ بِهِ مِنَ الأَعْداءِ
مِنْ مُهْجةٍ ذابَتْ أَسًى فَلَوَ انَّها
في العَيْنِ لَمْ يَمْنَعْ مِنَ الإغْفاءِ
لأَحدهم

Keep what you have left of me
for me
Perhaps one day
it will protect you
from your enemy
Keep whatever is left of a heart*
that pined away
with love-sickness
Were you to place my heart
in your eyes
It would not deprive you
of sleep

Anonymous

* "muhjah" (heart) also means soul, life, innermost self, blood-life etc.

تَعَجَّبُ أَنْ رأَتْ جِسْمي نَحيلاً
كَأَنَّ المَجْدَ يُدْرَكُ بِالصِّراعِ
أَبو تمَّام

She marveled
when she found me gaunt
as if glory
could only be attained
through struggle

Abū Tammām (d. 231/845)

أَلِفَ السُّقْمُ جِسْمَهُ وَالأَنينُ
وَبَراهُ الهَوى فَما يَسْتَبينُ
لا تَراهُ الظُّنونُ إلاَّ ظُنونًا
وَهْوَ أَخْفى مِنْ أَنْ تَراهُ الظُّنونُ
قَدْ سَمِعْنا أَنينَهُ مِنْ قَريب
فَاطْلُبوا الشَّخْصَ حَيْثُ كانَ الأَنينُ
لَمْ يَعِشْ إنَّهُ جَليدٌ وَلَكِنْ
ذابَ سُقْمًا فَلَمْ تَجِدْهُ المَنونُ
لأَحدهم

Lovesickness and moaning
have become intimate
with his body
and passion has so weakened him
that he could not be recognized
Doubts perceive him
only as uncertainties
yet he is too invisible
to be perceived by doubts
We have heard his moaning nearby,
So seek the body
where the moaning is
He is not alive,
Indeed, he is ice
that has melted
from love
so death could no longer
find him

Anonymous

أَلَمْ يرَ هَذا اللَّيْلُ عَيْنَيْكِ رُؤْيَتي
فَتَظْهَرَ فيهِ رِقَّةٌ وَنُحولُ
المتنبِّي

Had the night
not seen your eyes
as I saw them
so it would appear
thin and gaunt?

al-Mutanabbī (d.354/965)

أَشْبَهْتُ مِنْ أَجْلِه مَنْ كانَ يُشْبِهُهُ
وَكُلُّ شَيْءٍ مِنَ المَعْشوقِ مَعْشوقُ
حَتَّى حَكَيْتُ بِجِسْمي ما بِمُقْلَتِه
كَأَنَّ سُقْمِيَ مِنْ عَيْنَيْهِ مَسْروقُ
محمَّد بن يحيى الصُّولي

I resembled,
for the sake of my beloved,
whoever resembled him
Indeed, everything of one's beloved
is loved
I so resembled him
that my body copied
what was in his eyes
It was as though my lovesickness
had been stolen
from his eyes

Muḥammad ibn Yaḥyā al-Ṣūlī (d. 335/ 946 or 336/ 947)

شِعْرُ حَيٍّ أَتاكَ مِنْ لَفْظِ مَيْتٍ
صارَ بَيْنَ الحَياةِ وَالمَوْتِ وَقْفا
قَدْ بَرَتْهُ حَوادِثُ الدَّهْرِ حَتَّى
كانَ عَنْ أَعْيُنِ الحَوادِثِ يَخْفى
لَوْ تَأَمَّلْتَني لِتُثْبِتَ وَجْهي
لَمْ تُبِنْ مِنْ كِتابِ وَجْهِيَ حَرْفا
وَلَرَدَّدْتَ طَرْفَ عَيْنِكَ في جِسْمٍ
بَراهُ الصُّدودُ حَتَّى تَعَفَّى
أَبو نواس

Poetry of a living person
coming out of the breath
of a dying one,
standing still
between life and death
Time's misfortunes
have so worn him
that he has all but disappeared
from the sight
of time's misfortunes
Were you to gaze at me
to recognize my face
you would not distinguish
even a letter in the book
of my face
You would only be gazing at a body
so worn by rejection
that it has become effaced

Abū Nuwās (d.198/814)

On Love

كَأَنَّ قَطاةً عُلِّقَتْ بِجَناحِها
عَلى كَبِدي مِنْ شِدَّةِ الخَفَقانِ
وَإِنِّي لأَهْوى الحَشْرَ إِذْ قيلَ إِنَّني
وَعَفْراءَ يَوْمَ الحَشْرِ مُلْتَقِيانِ
عُرْوة بن حِزام

My heart was beating so hard,
It was as though a sand grouse *
had been hung
by its wings
on my heart
Indeed, I would long
for the day of resurrection
if I were told
that ʿAfrā' and I
would surely meet
there

ʿUrwah ibn Ḥizām (n.d.)

* It is said that sand grouse fly extreme distances to watering places to fetch water for their young. They soak themselves thoroughly in water, return the long distance without losing much of the water, and upon arrival flutter their wings fiercely over their young so they can drink. Altogether, this is a splendid simile to a hard-beating lovesick heart.

أَما عاهَدْتَني، يا قَلْبُ، أَنِّي
إذا ما تُبْتُ عَنْ لَيْلى تَتوبُ؟
فَها أَنا تائِبٌ عَنْ حُبِّ لَيْلى
فَما لَكَ كُلَّما ذُكِرَتْ تَذوبُ!
قيس بن المُلوَّح (مجنون ليلى)

Have you not promised me, O heart,
that if I repented of the love of Laylā
you too would repent?
Here I am!
I have repented of Laylā's love
How is it then that every time
Laylā's name is mentioned,
you melt away?

Majnūn Laylā (*Qays ibn al-Mulawwaḥ*) (*d. ca. 69/ 688*)

وَداعٍ دَعا إذْ نَحْنُ بِالخَيْفِ مِنْ مِنًى
فَهَيَّجَ أَحْزانَ الفُؤادِ وَما يَدْري
دَعا بِٱسْمِ لَيْلى غَيْرَها فَكَأَنَّما
أَطارَ بِلَيْلى طائِراً كانَ في صَدْري
مجنون ليلى

A crier,
when we were in al-Khayf,
near Minā,
called out names,
not knowing that he stirred sorrow
in my heart
He called out the name
of another Laylā
thus releasing a fluttering bird
that was in my heart

Majnūn Laylā (*d. ca. 69/ 688*)

كَأَنَّ القَلْبَ لَيْلَةَ قيلَ يُغْدى
بِلَيْلى العامِرِيَّةِ أَو يُراحُ
قَطاةٌ غَرَّها شَرَكٌ فَباتَتْ
تُنازِعُهُ وَقَدْ عَلِقَ الجَناحُ
قيس بنُ المُلَوَّح (مجنون ليلى)

It was as though my heart,
the night they said
that Laylā 'l-ʿĀmirīyah would depart,
were a sand grouse
lured by a snare
and struggling to pull away
its ensnared wings

Majnūn Laylā (*d. ca. 69/688*)

أَسِرْبَ القَطا هَلْ مَنْ يُعيرُ جَناحَهُ
لَعَلِّي إِلى مَنْ قَدْ هَوِيتُ أَطيرُ
لأحدهم

O covey of sand grouse!
Can any one of you
lend me your wings
perchance I might fly
to my beloved?

Anonymous

أَتاني هَواها قَبْلَ أَنْ أَعْرِفَ الهَوى
فَصادَفَ قَلْبًا خالِيًا فَتَمَكَّنا

ابْنُ الطثريَّة

Her love seized me
before I ever knew love
It found an empty heart
wherein it took hold

   Ibn al-Ṭathriyah (d. 127/ 744).

The line is also attributed to Majnūn Laylā and Dīk al-Jinn al-Ḥimṣī.

هَواها هَوًى لَمْ يَعْلَمِ القَلْبُ غَيْرَهُ
فَلَيْسَ لَهُ قَبْلٌ وَلَيْسَ لَهُ بَعْدُ

العَبَّاس بن الأَحنف

My heart has never known
any love but hers
Verily, there is no love
before or after
her love

   al-ʿAbbās ibn al-Aḥnaf (d. 193/ 808)

This line is noted for the best use of the two antonyms "*qabl*" (before) and "*baʿd*" (after).

أُقَلِّبُ طَرْفي في السَّماءِ لَعَلَّهُ
يُوافِقُ طَرْفي طَرْفَها حينَ تَنْظُرُ

جميل بن معمر

I turn my eyes
through the sky
Perhaps they will meet hers
when she looks up

   Jamīl Buthaynah (Jamīl ibn Maʿmar) (d. 82/ 701)

سَقَتْني بِعَيْنَيْها الهَوى وَسَقَيْتُها
فَدَبَّ دَبيبَ الخَمْرِ في كُلِّ مِفْصَلِ
سَلْم الخاسر

She gave me love to drink
with her eyes,
and likewise did I
Her love crept like wine
in every joint of mine

Salm al-Khāsir (n.d.)

Cf. "Drink to me only with thine eyes/ and I will pledge with mine." Ben Jonson (1572–1637)

وَلَوْلا دُموعي كَتَمْتُ الهَوى
وَلَوْلا الهَوى لَمْ تَكُنْ لي دُموعُ
لأحدهم

Had it not been for my tears
I would have concealed
my love
Had it not been for love
I would have had
no tears

Anonymous

كَأَنَّ فُؤَادي في مَخالِبِ طائِرٍ
إذا ذُكِرَتْ لَيْلى يَشُدُّ بِها قَبْضا
مجنون ليلى؟

It is as though my heart
were caught in the talons
of a bird
Whenever Laylā's name
is mentioned
the bird tightens its grip

Majnūn Laylā (d. ca. 69/ 688)

وَتَلَفَّتَتْ عَيْني فَمُذْ بَعُدَتْ
عَنِّي الطُّلولُ تَلَفَّتَ القَلْبُ
الشَّريف الرَّضي

My eyes looked back!
But when her abode
became distant
my heart looked back

Al-Sharīf al-Raḍī (d. 970/1016)

شَرِبْتُ الحُبَّ كَأْسًا بَعْدَ كَأْسٍ
فَما نَفَدَ الشَّرابُ ولا رَوِيتُ
لأَحدهم

I drank love
one cup after another
Neither was the drink finished
nor my thirst quenched

Anonymous

وَقَفْتُ عَلى رَبْعٍ لِمَيَّةَ نَاقَتي
فَمَا زِلْتُ أَبْكي عِنْدَهُ وَأُخاطِبُهْ
وَأَسْقيهِ حَتَّى كادَ مِمَّا أَبُثُّهُ
تُكَلِّمُني أَحْجارُهُ ومَلاعِبُهْ
ذو الرِّمَّة

I halted my mount
at Mayyah's abode
and cried,
addressing it,
watering it with my tears,
pouring out what was in my heart,
until the stones and the foreground
of her abode
nearly talked back
to me

Dhū 'l-Rummah (*d. 117/ 735*)

رَأَتْ قَمَرَ السَّماءِ فَذَكَّرَتْني
لَيالي وَصْلِنا بِالرَّقْمَتَيْنِ
كِلانا ناظِرٌ قَمَراً وَلَكِنْ
رَأَيْتُ بِعَيْنِها وَرَأَتْ بِعَيْني
القاضي عياض

She looked at the moon
reminding me of our reunion
at Raqmatayn
We both saw the same moon
But I saw it with her eyes
and she saw it with mine

al-Qāḍī ʿIyāḍ or ʿIyāḍ al-Qāḍī (d.544/1149)

عَشِيَّةَ ما لي حيلةٌ غَيْرَ أَنَّني
بِلَقْطِ الحَصى والخَطِّ في التُّرْبِ مُولَعُ
أَخُطُّ وأَمْحو الخَطَّ ثُمَّ أُعيدُهُ
بِكَفِّيَ والغُرْبانُ حَوْلِيَ خُشَّعُ
ذو الرِّمَّة

Many was the sunset
when I could do nothing
but gather pebbles
and passionately scribble
in the dust!
I would draw a line
erase it
draw another
erase it with my palm
while crows,
eyes cast down,
humbly perched
        around me

Dhū 'l-Rummah (*d. 117/ 735*)

The crow was known for its timidity; in this instance, the crows did not feel his presence because he was utterly dazed in a sad love stupor.

وأَخْرُجُ مِنْ بَيْنِ البُيوتِ لَعَلَّني
أُحَدِّثُ عَنْكِ النَّفْسَ في السِّرِّ خالِيَا
قيس بن ذَريح

I slip out
from amongst the tents
Perhaps being alone
I can secretly talk
to myself
about you

Qays ibn Dharīḥ (*d. 68/ 687*)

وَإِنِّي وَتَهْيامي بِعَزَّةَ بَعْدَما
تَخَلَّيْتُ عَمَّا بَيْنَنا وَتَخَلَّتِ
لَكالمُرْتَجي ظِلَّ الغَمامةِ كُلَّما
تَبَوَّأَ مِنْها لِلْمَقيلِ ٱضْمَحَلَّت
كُثَيِّر عَزَّة

I, in my desperate love for ʿAzzah,
after she and I had severed
what was between us,
am like one who hopes for shade
from a cloud that clears away
as soon as he settles down
to rest

Kuthayyir ʿAzzah (d. 105/ 723)

فَما بَلَغَ الدَّمْعُ الّذي كُنْتُ أَرْتَجي
ولا فَعَلَ الوَجْدُ الّذي خِلْتُ يَفْعَلُ
وَما كُلُّ نيرانِ الجَوى تُحْرِقُ الحَشا
ولا كُلُّ أَدْواءِ الصَّبابةِ تَقْتُلُ
البُحْتُري

The tears I had hoped for
failed to flow
nor has love done
what I thought
it would do
The fires of love do not always
burn the heart
nor do all ills of love smart

al-Buḥturī (d. 284/ 897)

صَحا قَلْبُهُ عَنْها عَلى أَنَّ ذِكْرَةً
إذا خَطَرَتْ دارَتْ بِهِ الأَرْضُ قَائما
المُرَقِّش الأَصْغَر

His heart has awakened
from her love
But whenever he remembered her
the earth would turn around
and around with him

al-Muraqqash al-Aṣghar (*n.d.*)

تَكادُ يَدي تَنْدى إذا ما لَمَسْتُها
وَيَنْبُتُ في أَطْرافِها الوَرَقُ النَّضْرُ
وَإنِّي لَتَعْرُوني لِذِكْراكِ هِزَّةٌ
كَما ٱنْتَفَضَ العُصْفورُ بَلَّلَهُ القَطْرُ
أَبو صخر الهُذَلي

My hand almost becomes dewy
when I touch her
and green leaves sprout
on its fingertips
A shudder seizes me
whenever her name
is mentioned
just as a bird shudders
when drenched
in a rain shower

Abū Ṣakhr al-Hudhalī (*d. 2nd half of seventh century A.D.*)

يَلُومُ في الحُبِّ مَنْ لَمْ يَدْرِ طَعْمَ هَوًى
وَإِنَّما يَعْذُرُ العُشَّاقَ مَنْ عَشِقا
الباخرزي أو أَحمد بن داوُد

Those who have not savored love
blame those who have
But lovers forgive those
who are in love

al-Bākharzī (d. 658/1259)

دَعْني وَشُرْبَ الهَوى يا شاربَ الكاسِ
فَإِنَّني لِلَّذي حَسَّيْتَهُ حاسِي
أبو تمَّام

Let me drink love, O tippler!
for we are both sipping
the same drink

Abū Tammām (d. 231/ 845)

أَجِدُ الملامةَ في هَواكِ لَذيذةً
كَلَفًا بِذِكْرِكِ فَلْيَلُمْنِي اللُّوَّمُ
محمَّد بن عبد الله بن رزين أَبي الشِّيص

They blame me for loving you!
How sweet the blame!
So long as they mention your name
let them blame
and blame away

Muḥammad ibn ʿAbdallah ibn Razīn Abī al-Shīṣ (d. 196/ 811)

صَبَبْتِ هَواكِ عَلى قَلْبِه
فَضاقَ وَأَعْلَنَ ما قَدْ كَتَمْ
بشَّار بن بُرد

You poured your love
on his heart!
His heart contracted
and poured out
all it had concealed

Bashshār ibn Burd (*d. 167/784*)

لَمْ يُبْقِ مِنِّي حُبُّها ما خلا
حُشاشَةً في بَدَنٍ ناحِلِ
يا مَنْ رأَى قَبْلي قَتيلاً بَكى
مِنْ شِدَّةِ الوَجْدِ عَلى القاتِلِ
أبو العتاهية

My love for her has left of me
but a last breath
in a gaunt body
Oh! whosoever before me
has seen a slain lover
who passionately weeps
over his slayer?

Abū 'l-ʿAtāhiyah (*d. 210/ 825*)

يَموتُ الهَوى مِنِّي إذا ما لَقِيتُها
وَيَحْيا إذا فارَقْتُها فيَعودُ
جميل بُثَينة

My love for her dies
whenever we meet
But is revived

and returns to me
whenever we part

Jamīl Buthaynah (d. 82 /701)

وَما عَجَبي مَوْتُ المُحِبِّينَ في الهَوى
وَلَكِنْ بَقاءُ العاشِقينَ عَجيبُ
عُرْوة بن حزام

Lovers dying of love
is no surprise to me
Lovers staying alive
is truly a surprise
to me

ʿ*Urwah ibn Ḥizām* (n.d.)

أَرَقَّ نَسيبي فيه رِقَّةَ حُسْنه
فَلَمْ أَدْرِ أيٌّ قَبْلَها مِنهُما السِّحْرُ
وَطِبْنا مَعًا ثَغْراً وَشِعْراً كَأَنَّما
لَهُ مَنْطِقي ثَغْرٌ وَلي ثَغْرُهُ شِعْرُ
ابن خَفاجة

My love poetry for him
made his graceful beauty
more elegant
I know not which charming elegance
came first
We have sported with each other,
mouth and poetry,
as though my poetry were his mouth
and his mouth my poetry

Ibn Khafājah (d. 533/1138)

يَوْمٌ أَفاضَ جَوًى أَغاضَ تَعَزِّيًا
خاضَ الهَوى بَحْرَيْ حِجاهُ المُزْبِدِ
أَبو تمَّام

The day overflowed with passion
and receded into solace
Love has plunged
into the two seas
of his vigorous wit

Abū Tammām (*d. 231/845*)

The Arabic original of this line was cited as an example of convoluted interdependence of words, which complexity has led to obfuscation.

تَداوَيْتُ مِنْ لَيْلى بِلَيْلى فَما اشْتَفى
بِماءِ الرُّبى مَنْ باتَ بِالماءِ يَشْرَقُ
البُحْتُري

I tried to cure myself from Laylā
with Laylā
But he who chokes on water
cannot be cured
with highland water

al-Buḥturī (*d. 284/ 897*)

On Soul-Melting Love

لَيْسَ ذا الدَّمْعُ دَمْعَ عَيْني وَلَكِنْ
هِيَ نَفْسي تُذيبُها أَنْفاسي
ديك الجنّ الحمصي

These tears are not
the tears of my eyes
but rather my soul
dissolved
by my breath

Dīk al-Jinn al-Ḥimṣī (*d. 235/ 849*)

إنَّ نَفْسي تَذوبُ في كُلِّ يَوْم
حَسَراتٍ وَمِنْ جُفوني تَسيلُ
الخُبْزَرُزِّي

My soul melts away
for sorrow every day
and gushes forth
from my eye

Khubzarzī (*Khubz 'aruzzī*) (*d.328/ 939*)

وَلَيْسَ الّذي يَجْري مِنَ العَيْنِ مَاءَها
وَلَكِنَّهُ نَفْسٌ تَذوبُ فَتَقْطُرُ
الجَهْمي

These are not tears
flowing from my eyes
It is my soul
that has melted
and is dripping
away

al-Jahmī or ʿAlī ibn al-Jahm (*d. 249/863*)

دَمْعي جَرى مِنْ جُفوني يَوْمَ بَيْنِهِمُ
فَلَسْتُ أدْري أدَمْعي كانَ أَمْ رُوحي
العُجَيفي الكُوفي

My tears gushed forth
the day they departed
I do not know
if what flowed
was my tears
or my soul

al-ʿUjayfī al-Kūfī (*n.d.*)

The word "they" can be understood as "she."

حُشاشَتي وَدَّعَتْني يَوْمَ بَيْنِهِمُ
وَشَيَّعَتْهُمْ وَخَلَّتْني وَأَحْزاني
وَقَدْ أَشارُوا بِتَسْليم عَلى حَذَرٍ
مِنَ الرَّقيبِ بِأَطْرافٍ وَأَجْفانِ
بشّار بن بُرد

My last breath bade farewell to me
and accompanied them
the day they departed
leaving me to my sorrow
Wary of the guardian
they bade farewell to me
with their eyelids
and glances

Bashshār ibn Burd (*d. 167/784*)

The words "they" and "their" refer to "she" and "her."

حُشاشةُ نَفْسٍ وَدَّعَتْ يَوْمَ وَدَّعُوا
فَلَمْ أَدْرِ أَيَّ الظّاعِنَيْنِ أُشَيِّعُ
أَشارُوا بِتَسْليمٍ فَجُدْنا بِأَنْفُسٍ
تَسيلُ مِنَ الآماقِ والسَّمُ أَدْمُعُ
المتنبّي

My last breath bade farewell to me
the day they departed
I know not which of the departed
I should bid farewell to
They saluted farewell
and I returned it
with my soul lavishly streaming
from the corners
of my eyes

al-Mutanabbī (*d. 354/965*)

On Ṣūfī Love

أَنا مَنْ أَهْوى وَمَنْ أَهْوى أَنا
نَحْنُ رُوحانِ حَلَلْنا بَدَنَا
نَحْنُ مُذْ كُنَّا عَلى عَهْدِ الهَوى
تُضْرَبُ الأَمْثالُ لِلنَّاسِ بِنَا
فإذا أَبْصَرْتَني أَبْصَرْتَهُ
وإذا أَبْصَرْتَهُ أَبْصَرْتَنا
أَيُّها السَّائِلُ عَنْ قِصَّتنا
لَوْ تَرانا لَمْ تُفَرِّقْ بَيْنَنا
الحَلاَّج

I am whom I love
and the one I love is I
We are two souls
in one body*
People have followed our example
for as long as love has been
If you see me
you have seen Him
And if you see Him
you have seen the two of us
You who wonder about our state,
were you to see us,
you could not distinguish
between us

al-Ḥusayn ibn Manṣūr al-Ḥallāj (d. 309/922)

* *"Ḥalalnā"* ("in one body" is from *ḥulūl* which in ṣūfī terminologi is union with God.

لَقَدْ صارَ قَلْبي قابِلاً كُلَّ صُورةٍ
فَمَرْعًى لِغُزْلانٍ وَدَيْرٌ لِرُهْبانِ
وَبَيْتٌ لأَوْثانٍ وَكَعْبةُ طائِفٍ
وَأَلْواحُ تَوْراةٍ وَمِصْحَفُ قُرآنِ
أَدينُ بِدِينِ الحُبِّ أَنَّى تَوَجَّهَتْ
رَكائِبُهُ فالحُبُّ دِيني وَإيْماني
ابن عربي

My heart is capable of every form:
a pasture for gazelles,
a cloister for monks,
a fane for idols,
a Kaʿbah for pilgrims,
the tables of the Torah
and the Qur'ān
Love is the faith I hold
wherever its mounts turn
Love is my religion
and my faith

Muḥyī al-Dīn ibn al-ʿArabī (d.638/ 1240)

Translated by R. A. Nicholson in *A Literary History of the Arabs*, p. 403.

رُوحُهُ رُوحي وَرُوحي رُوحُهُ
مَنْ رأى رُوحَيْنِ حَلَّتْ بَدَنا
الحَلاَّج

His soul is my soul
and my soul is His
Whoever has seen two souls
in one body?

al-Ḥusayn ibn Manṣūr al-Ḥallāj (d. 309/922)

On the Phantom of the Beloved

أَجِدَّكَ ما يَنْفَكُّ يَسْرِي لِزَيْنَبَا
خَيَالٌ إِذا آبَ الظَّلامُ تَأَوَّبَا
سَرى مِنْ أَعالِي الشَّام يَجْلُبُهُ الكَرى
هُبُوبَ نَسِيمِ الرَّوْضِ تَجْلُبُهُ الصَّبَا
البحتري

Verily, Zaynab's phantom
never ceases to visit
Whenever darkness returns
It arrives:
night-journeyed
from the heights of Damascus
borne by sleep
like the soughing
of the garden breeze
borne by the east wind

al-Buḥturī (d. 284/897)

This line and three others by al-Buḥturī moved the critic ʿAbd al-Qāhir al-Jurjānī to critical exuberance. See *The Neckveins of Winter*, p. 35

لَمْ يَطُلْ لَيْلِي وَلَكِنْ لَمْ أَنَمْ
وَنَفى عَنِّي الكَرى طَيْفٌ أَلَمّ
خَفِّفِي يا عَبْدُ عَنِّي وَٱعْلَمِي
أَنَّني يا عَبْدُ مِنْ لَحْمٍ وَدَمْ
إِنَّ في بُرْدَيَّ جِسْمًا ناحِلاً
لَوْ تَوَكَّأْتِ عَلَيْهِ لانْهَدَمْ
بشّار بن بُرْد

My night was not long!
I just had no sleep,
because her phantom
alighted on me
banishing my sleep
Have pity on me, O ʿAbdah,
and know that I am merely a man
of flesh and blood
My clothes contain
but an emaciated body,
were you to lean on it
it would surely
collapse

Bashshār ibn Burd (d. 168/784)

Bashshār ibn Burd was blind, and it is related that he was obese and pockmarked.

زارَ الخَيالُ نَحِيلاً مِثْلَ مُرْسِلِهِ
فَما شَفانِيَ مِنْهُ الضَّمُّ والقُبَلُ
ما زارَنِي قَطُّ إلاَّ كَي يُوافِقَنِي
عَلى الرُّقادِ فَيَنْفِيهِ وَيَرْتَحِلُ
إبن القطّان

فأَكمل البَيْتَيْن الحَيْص بَيْص:
وَما دَرى أَنَّ نَوْمِي حِيلةٌ نُصِبَتْ
لِطَيْفِهِ حِينَ أَعْيا اليَقْظَةَ الحِيَلُ

Her phantom, slender
as its sender,
visited me
Embracing and kissing it
was not a cure
for me
Her phantom visited me
only to conspire with me
against sleep
so it could banish sleep
and then depart
But her phantom was unaware
that my sleep was but a ruse
I had set for it
after all ruses
had baffled wakefulness

The first two lines are by Ibn al- Qaṭṭān (d. 559/1163), a poet from Baghdad. The last line, composed in completion of the idea-image of the first two lines, in a friendly challenge as requested by the vizier-patron, is by al-Ḥayṣ Bayṣ (d. 575/1179).

قالَتْ لِطَيْفِ خَيالٍ زارَني وَمَضى:
بِاللهِ صِفْهُ ولا تُنْقِصْ ولا تَزِدِ
فَقالَ: خَلَّفْتُهُ لَوْ ماتَ مِنْ ظَمَإٍ
وَقُلْتِ: «قِفْ عَنْ وُرُودِ الْمَاءِ لَمْ يَرِدِ
الوأواء الدِّمشقي

She said to her phantom
as it set off to visit me:
By God, describe him:
no more, no less,
Her phantom said:
I left him in such a state
that were he nearly dying
of thirst
and you said:
"stop seeking water"
he would not seek water

al-Wa' wā' al-Dimashqī (d. ca. 385/995)

On Wine and Drinking

أعاذِلَ، لَوْ شَرِبْتَ الخَمْرَ حَتَّى
يَظَلَّ لِكُلِّ أُنْمُلَةٍ دَبيبُ
إِذًا لَعَذَرْتَني وَعَلِمْتَ أَنِّي
لِما أَتْلَفْتُ مِنْ مالي مُصيبُ
إياس بن الأَرَثّ

If she should chide me, I would say:
Ah, had you raised the brimming cup
to taste its fragrance with your lips,
and felt the warm blood pulsing up,
tingling your very fingertips,
Then you would deem my passion right
to spend my cash in such delight.

Iyās ibn al-Araṯṯ (n.d.)

(British translation)

تَداوَيْتُ عَنْ لَيْلى بِلَيْلى مِنَ الهَوى
كَما يَتَداوى شارِبُ الْخَمْرِ بِالْخَمْرِ
مجنون ليلى (قيس بن المُلَوَّح)

I cured myself from love of Laylā
with Laylā
just as a toper cures himself
with wine

Majnūn Laylā (d. 68/687)

وَكَأْسٍ شَرِبْتُ عَلى لَذَّةٍ
وَأُخْرى تَداوَيْتُ مِنْها بِها
لِكَيْ يَعْلَمَ النَّاسُ أَنِّي ٱمْرُؤٌ
أَتَيْتُ الفُتُوَّةَ مِنْ بابِها
الأَعشى

One cup I quaffed for pleasure
and then another
for cure
So people may know
that I am youthful, generous
and chivalrous too

al-Aʿshā (d. 7/628)

دَعْ عَنْكَ لَوْمي فَإِنَّ اللَّوْمَ إِغْراءُ
وَداوِني بِالَّتي كانَتْ هِيَ الدَّاءُ
أَبو نُوَاس

Blame me not
for blame is temptation
But rather cure me
with what was
my malady

Abū Nuwās (d. 198/814)

أَلا فَاْسْقِنِي خَمْراً وَقُلْ لي هِيَ الخَمْرُ
ولا تَسْقِنِي سِراً إِذا أَمْكَنَ الجَهْرُ
أَبو نُواس

Ho! a cup, and fill it up,
and tell me it is wine
For I will never drink in shade
if I can drink in shine

Abū Nuwās (d. 198/814)

Translated by R. A. Nicholson, in *A Literary History of the Arabs*, p. 295

فَكُلُّ كَفٍّ رآها ظَنَّها قَدَحًا
وَكُلُّ شَخْصٍ رآهُ ظَنَّهُ السَّاقي
أَبو نُواس

He thought every hand he saw
a cup
and every person
a cup-bearer

Abū Nuwās (d. 198/814)

تَوَهَّمْتُها في كَأْسِها فَكَأَنَّما
تَوَهَّمْتُ شَيْئًا لَيْسَ يُدْرِكُ بِالْعَقْلِ
أَبو نُواس

It was as though I had envisioned
something imperceptible
when I envisioned it
in a cup

Abū Nuwās (d. 198/814)

كَيْفَ النُّزوعُ عَنِ الصِّبا وَالْكاسِ
قِسْ ذا لَنا، يا عاذِلي، بِقِياسِ
قَالُوا: كَبِرْتَ، فَقُلْتُ: ما كَبِرَتْ يَدي
عَنْ أَنْ تَخُبَّ إِلى فَمي بِالْكاسِ
أبو نُواس

How can I,
O you who rebuke me,
abstain from youthful pleasures
and drinking
Apply your logic* to that
if you can
They tell me, "You have grown old,"
But I say "not too old for my hand
to amble to my mouth
with a cup."

Abū Nuwās (d. 198/814)

*"Logic," *lit., qiyās* (reasoning by analogy) is the fourth foundation of Islamic jurisprudence.

إِذا مُتُّ فَادْفُنّي إِلى جَنْبِ كَرْمَةٍ
تُرَوِّي عِظامي بَعْدَ مَوْتي عُرُوقَها
ولا تَدْفُنَنِّي في الفَلاةِ فَإِنَّني
أَخافُ إِذا ما مُتُّ أَلاَّ أَذُوقَها
أَبو مِحْجَن الثَّقَفِيّ

Friend, bury me, when I die, a stock of the vine beside,
That after my death its roots may moisten my thirsty bones.
And bury me not amidst the desert, for lo, I fear
Lest when I am dead I ne'er shall taste of it evermore.

Abū Miḥjan al-Thaqafī (d. ca. 30/ 650)

Translated by R. A. Nicholson in *Translations of Eastern Poetry and Prose*, p. 64.

ما الْعَيْشُ إِلاَّ في جُنونِ الصِّبا
فَإِنْ تَوَلّى فَجُنونُ المُدامْ
محمَّد بن عطيَّة العطوي

Life is naught
but the madness of youth
But if youth fades away
then it is the madness
of wine

Muḥammad ibn ʿAṭiyyah al-ʿAṭwī (n.d.)

أُتْرُكِ الأَطْلالَ لا تَعْبَأْ بِها
إِنَّها مِنْ كُلِّ بُؤْسٍ دانِيَهْ
وَٱشْرَبِ الرّاحَ عَلى تَحْريمِها
إِنَّما دُنْياكَ دارٌ فانِيَهْ
مِنْ عُقارٍ مَنْ رَآها قالَ لي:
صِيدَتِ الشَّمْسُ لَنا في آنِيَهْ
أَبو نُواس

Abandon desert encampments!
Pay them no heed,
for they are close to all misery
Describe wine, instead,
though it is proscribed
This world is but
a transient abode
So drink wine,
described to me
by whoever sees it,
as the sun captured
in a vessel

Abū Nuwās (d. 198/814)

لا أَشْرَبُ الرَّاحَ إِلاَّ مِنْ يَدَيْ رَشَإٍ
تَقْبيلُ راحتِهِ أَشْهى مِنَ الرَّاحِ
إسحاق المَوْصِليّ

I only drink wine
from the hand of a young boy*
kissing his palm
is more coveted
than the wine

Isḥāq al-Mawṣilī (d. 236/850)

* *Lit.*, fawn able to walk.

لَأَحْسَنُ مِنْ قَرْعِ المَثاني وَرَجْعِها
تَواتُرُ صَوْتِ الثَّغْرِ يُقْرَعُ بِالثَّغْرِ
وَسُكْرُ الهَوى أَرْوى لِعَظْمي وَمَفْصِلي
مِنَ الشُّرْبِ في الْكاساتِ مِنْ عاتِقِ الخَمْرِ
إسحاق المَوْصِليّ

The unbroken sound
of one mouth kissing another
is more pleasant to me
than the strumming
of a lute
And the inebriation of love
better quenches my bones and joints
than drinking aged wine
in fresh cups

Isḥāq al-Mawṭilī (d. 236/850)

On Beauty

كَأَنَّ ثِيابَهُ أَطْلَعْنَ
مِنْ أَزْرارِهِ قَمَرا
يَزيدُكَ وَجْهُهُ حُسْنًا
إذا ما زِدْتَهُ نَظَرا
أبو نواس

It is as though his clothes,
through the buttons,
had revealed a full moon
The longer you look at his face
the more beautiful you become

Abū Nuwās (d. 198 /813)

لا تَعْجَبوا مِنْ بِلى غِلالَتِه
قَدْ زَرَّ أَزْرارَهُ عَلى القَمَرِ
ابن المُعْتَزّ

Marvel not at the shabbiness
of his garments
for he has fastened his buttons
on the moon

Ibn al-Muʿtazz (d. 296 /908)

وَأَثْقَلَها الحُسْنُ الّذي قَدْ تَكاثَرَتْ
مَلاحَتُهُ حَتَّى تَثَنَّتْ مِنَ الثِّقْلِ
ابن سَناء المُلْك

Her graceful abundant beauty
has so weighed her down
that it bent her low

Ibn Sanā' al-Mulk (d. 608/1211)

قامَتْ تُظَلِّلُني مِنَ الشَّمْسِ
نَفْسٌ أَعَزُّ عَلَيَّ مِنْ نَفْسي
قامَتْ تُظَلِّلُني وَمِنْ عَجَبٍ
شَمْسٌ تُظَلِّلُني مِنَ الشَّمْسِ!
ابن العميد

She set out to shade me
from the sun,
a sun
dearer to me
than my soul
Oh how wonderful!
a sun shading me
from the sun

Ibn al-ʿAmīd (d. 360/ 970)

Arabs compare a woman's beautiful face to the sun (feminine) or to the moon (masculine) if it is bright, round, brilliant , unattainable etc.

إذا ارْتَعَشَتْ خافَ الجَبانُ ارْتِعاشَها
وَمَنْ يُعَلَّقْ حَيْثُ عُلِّقَ يَفْرَقِ
النابغة الذبياني

Were she to wear earrings,
the cowardly earrings would fear;
Indeed, whoever dangled
from where they are
would certainly show fear

al-Nābighah al-Dhubyānī (d. 604 A.D.)

The poet is describing a woman's long neck, a feature of great beauty.

بَعيدةُ مَهْوى القُرْطِ...
عمر بن أَبي ربيعة

Deep is the abyss
below her earrings

Umar ibn Abī Rabīʿah (d. 94/712)

The poet is referring to her long neck.

كأَنَّ المُدامَ وَصَوْبَ الغَمام
وَريحَ الخُزامى ونَشْرَ القُطُرْ
يُعَلُّ بِهِ بَرْدُ أَنْيابِها
إذا غَرَّدَ الطَّائِرُ المُسْتَحِرْ
امرؤ القيس

It is as if wine,
the downpour of rain clouds,
the scent of lavender and aloes-wood
had drenched her cool teeth
when the dawn birds
warbled

Imru' al-Qays (d. 545 A.D.)

بِمُخَضَّبٍ رَخْصٍ كأَنَّ بَنانَهُ
عَنَمٌ يَكادُ مِنَ اللَّطافةِ يُعْقَدُ
النابغة

[She picked up the headscarf]
with a soft hennaed hand,
with fingers like vine tendrils
so supple
they could almost
be tied

al-Nābighah al-Dhubyānī (d. 604 A.D.)

لَبِسْنَ الْوَشْيَ لا مُتَجَمِّلاتٍ
وَلَكِنْ كَي يَصُنَّ بِهِ الجَمالا
وَضَفَّرْنَ الغدائِرَ لا لِحُسْنٍ
وَلَكِنْ خِفْنَ في الشَّعْرِ الضَّلالا
المتنبِّي

They wore silk brocades,
not to adorn themselves
but to protect their beauty
And they plaited their hair
not for elegance
but for fear that eyes
might become lost
in it

al-Mutanabbī (d. 354/965)

يَتَرَشَّفْنَ مِنْ فَمي رَشَفاتٍ
هُنَّ فيهِ أَحْلى مِنَ التَّوْحيدِ
المتنبّي

They drink
from my mouth
sips sweeter
than tawḥīd

al-Mutanabbī (d. 354/965)

* Tawḥīd in Islam is profession of faith in the oneness of God; tawḥīd is also a kind of date, which is used in this line to avoid obvious blasphemy.

لَو أَسْنَدَتْ مَيْتًا إلى نَحْرِها
عاشَ وَلَمْ يُنْقَلْ إلى قابِرِ
الأَعشى

Were she to prop a dead man
on her neck
he would live again
and not have
to be interred

al-Aʿshā (d. 7/629)

On Soft Skin

وَرِقَّةُ وَجْهٍ لَوْ خَتَمْتَ بِنَظْرَةٍ
عَلى وَجْنَتَيْهِ ما ٱمَّحى أَثَرُ الخَتْمِ
اَلمتنبِّي

So soft is his face!
Were you to imprint a glance
on his cheeks
the imprint would not be
effaced

al-Mutanabbī (d. 354/965)

وَإِذا تَوَهَّمَ أَنْ يَراها ناظِرٌ
تَرَكَ التَّوَهُّمُ جِسْمَها مَكْلوما
لأَحدهم

If one were only to fancy
looking at her
His imagination would leave
her body wounded

Anonymous

يَكادُ فَضيضُ الماءِ يَخْدِشُ جِلْدَها
إذا ٱغْتَسَلَتْ بالماءِ مِنْ رِقَّةِ الجِلْدِ
وَلَوْ لَبِسَتْ ثَوْبًا مِنَ الوَرْدِ خَالِصًا
لَخَدَّشَ مِنْ جِلْدٍ لَها وَرَقُ الوَرْدِ
يُثَقِّلُها لُبْسُ الحَريرِ لِلينِها
وَتَشْكو إلى جَاراتِها ثِقَلَ العِقْدِ
وَأَرْحَمُ خَدَّيْها إذا ما لَحَظْتُها
حَذاراً لِلَحْظي أَنْ يُؤَثِّرَ في الخَدِّ
قيس بن ذَريح

So delicate is her skin!
Were she to sprinkle herself with water,
the droplets would scratch her skin
And were she to wear
a robe of pure white roses
the rose petals would scratch her skin
So supple is she
that wearing silk
weighs her down
And she complains to her female neighbors
about the weight of her necklace
I pity her cheeks
if I glance at her
for fear that my glance
would leave a mark
on her cheeks

Qays ibn Dharīḥ (d. 68/ 687)

The first line with "*faḍīḍ*" (sprinkle of water) instead of "*ḥubāb*" (droplets of water) is also attributed to Majnūn Laylā (d. 69/ 688)

مِنَ القاصِراتِ الطَّرْفِ لَوْ دَبَّ مُحْوِلٌ
مِنَ الذَّرِّ فَوْقَ الإِتْبِ مِنْها لأَثَّرا
امرؤ القَيْس

Many a pudical woman,
were small ants to crawl
on her shirt,
they would leave a mark
on her skin

Imru' al-Qays (d. ca. 545 A.D.)

فَلَوْ دَرَجَ النَّمْلُ الصِّغارُ بِجِلْدِها
لأَنْدَبَ أَعْلى جِلْدِها مَدْرَجُ النَّمْلِ
جميل بن عبد الله بن مَعْمَر العُذْري

If small ants were to crawl
on her skin
They would leave wounds
in their track

Jamīl ibn Maʿmar al-ʿUdhrī (d. ca. 82/ 701)

وَخَصْرٌ تَثْبُتُ الأَبْصارُ فيهِ
كَأَنَّ عَلَيْهِ مِنْ حَدَقٍ نِطاقا
المتنبِّي

It was as though gazes
fixed on her waist
have formed a girdle
for her waist

al-Mutanabbī (d. 354/965)

يَجْرَحُهُ اللَّحْظُ بِتَكْرارِهِ
وَيَشْتَكي الإِيماءَ بِالكَفِّ
لأَحدهم (مُحْدَث)

If you looked at him
time and again
your gaze would injure him
And if you motioned to him
he would complain

Anonymous

تَوَهَّمَهُ قَلْبي فَأَصْبَحَ خَدُّهُ
وَفيهِ مَكانُ الوَهْمِ مِنْ نَظَري أَثْرُ
وَمَرَّ بِفِكْري خاطِراً فَجَرَحْتُهُ
وَلَمْ أَرَ جِسْمًا قَطُّ يَجْرَحُهُ الفِكْرُ
وَصافَحَهُ قَلْبي فَآلَمَ كَفَّهُ
فَمِنْ غَمْزِ قَلْبي في أَنامِلِهِ عَقْرُ
أبو نواس

My soul envisioned his cheeks
leaving a mark thereon
He crossed my mind,
as merely a thought,
and he was wounded
I have never seen a body
being injured by a mere thought
My heart embraced his hand
his hand hurt
My heart's touch
left a mark
on his fingertips

Abū Nuwās (d. 198 /814)

يا مَنْ لِقَلْبٍ صِيغَ مِنْ صَخْرةٍ
في جَسَدٍ مِنْ لُؤْلُؤٍ رَطْبِ
جَرَحْتُ خَدَّيْهِ بِلَحْظي فَما
بَرِحْتُ حَتَّى ٱقْتَصَّ مِنْ قَلْبي
إبراهيم بن المهدي

O beloved, whose heart
is formed of stone,
whose body is of delicate pearl
I wounded his cheeks
by looking at him
and kept looking
until he took revenge
on my heart

Ibrāhīm ibn al-Mahdī (d. 225/839)

أَدْمَيْتُ بِاللَّحَظاتِ وَجْنَتَهُ
فَٱقْتَصَّ ناظِرُهُ مِنَ القَلْبِ
أَحمد بن أَبي قَنَن (اقتبسه من المهدي)

I gazed at his cheeks
until they bled
So his eyes took revenge
on my heart

Aḥmad ibn Abī Qanan (n.d.)

The critics noted that Abī Qanan plagiarized al-Mahdī's line, above.

مَرَّ بِنا وَالعُيونُ تَرْمُقُهُ
تَجْرَحُ مِنْهُ مَواضِعَ القُبَلِ
أُفْرِغَ في قالَبِ الجَمالِ فَما
يَصْلُحُ إلاّ لِذاكَ العَمَلِ
أبو نواس

He passed by us
and eyes began gazing at him
injuring all his kissable parts
He was cast
into the mold of beauty
and cannot be
but beautiful

Abū Nuwās (d. 198/814)

بِمُخَضَّبٍ رَخْصٍ كَأَنَّ بَنانَهُ
عَنَمٌ يَكادُ مِنَ اللَّطافةِ يُعْقَدُ
النابغة الذبياني

Her fingers are like tendrils
of vine
so delicate that they can almost
be tied

al-Nābighah al-Dhubyānī (d. 604 A.D.)

On Eyes and Tears

أَتَتْني تُؤَنِّبُني بِالْبُكا
فَأَهْلاً بِها وَبِتَأْنِيبِها
تَقولُ وَفي قَوْلِها حِشْمَةٌ:
أَتَبْكي بِعَيْنٍ تَراني بِها؟
فَقُلْتُ: إِذا ٱسْتَحْسَنَتْ غَيْرَكُمْ
أَمَرْتُ الدُّموعَ بِتَأْديبِها

لأَحدهم

She came to me
chiding me for crying
She and her rebukes
are most welcome
Blushing, she said:
Do you cry with the same eyes
you see me with?
I said to her:
If my eyes were to admire
anyone else but you
I would order my tears
to discipline my eyes

Anonymous

فَأَنْتَ الّذي أَشْرَقْتَ عَيْني بِمائها
وَعَلَّمْتَها بِالْهَجْرِ أَنْ تَهْجُرَ الغَمْضا
وَأَغْرَيْتَها بِالدَّمْعِ حَتَّى جُفونُها
لَتُنْكِرُ مِنْ فَقْدِ الكَرى بَعْضَها بَعْضا
فَإِنْ كانَ لا يُرْضيكَ إِلاَّ مَنِيَّتي
وَطالَتْ حَياتي لِلشَّقا فَمَتى تَرْضى؟
لأَحدهم

It was you who made my eyes
choke on their tears
and, parting, you taught my eyes
to part with sleep
You so seduced my eyes with tears
that their lids,
for lack of sleep,
have renounced each other
If only my death would satisfy you
after a long lifetime of misery
Would you then be satisfied?

Anonymous

إِنْ زَنَتْ عَيْنُهُ بِغَيْرِكَ فَاضْرِبْها
بِطُولِ السُّهادِ وَالدَّمْعِ حَدَّا
ابن المُعْتَزّ

If his eyes commit adultery
by looking at someone else
Lash* them with tears
and long sleeplessness

Ibn al-Muʿtazz (d. 296/908)

* Lit., "Give them the *ḥadd* puishment", which, in Islamic Law, is eighty lashes.

لَيْتَني إِذْ أَراهُ كُلِّي عُيونٌ
فَبِعَيْنَيْنِ لَسْتُ أَشْبَعُ مِنْهُ
لأَحدهم

I wish I could become
all eyes
when I see him
for I can not see enough of him
with only two eyes

Anonymous

إِنَّ العُيونَ الَّتي في طَرْفِها حَوَرٌ
قَتَلْنَنا ثُمَّ لَمْ يُحْيِينَ قَتْلانا
يَصْرَعْنَ ذا اللُّبِّ حَتّى لا حَراكَ لَهُ
وَهُنَّ أَضْعَفُ خَلْقِ اللهِ إنْسانا
جرير

Fair black eyes
have smitten us
Yet, they refuse
to revive us
They smite a lover's heart
until it becomes motionless
though, of all God's creatures,
they are the weakest

Jarīr (d. 110/ 728)

رامِياتٍ بأَسْهُمٍ رِيشُها الهُدْبُ
تَشُقُّ القُلوبَ قَبْلَ الجُلُودِ
المتنبِّي

Their eyes cast arrows
whose vanes, the eyelashes,
pierce the heart
before the skin

al-Mutanabbī (d. 354/965)

رَمَتْني بِسَهْمٍ رِيشُهُ الكُحْلُ لم يَجُزْ
ظَواهِرَ جِلْدي وَهْوَ في القَلْبِ جارِحُ
كُثَيِّر

She cast at me an arrow
whose vanes, black eyelashes,
did not go past the skin
yet, they wounded
my heart

Kuthayyir ʿAzzah (d. 105/723)

وَأَسْبَلَتْ لُؤْلُؤًا مِنْ نَرْجِسٍ وَسَقَتْ
وَرْدًا وَعَضَّتْ عَلى العُنَّابِ بِالبَرَدِ
الوأْواء الدِّمشقي

She shed pearls
from narcissus,
watering roses,
and biting on jujube
with hailstones*

al-Wa'wā' al-Dimashqī (d. ca. 385/995)

* "Pearls" are tears; "narcissus" are eyes; "roses" are cheeks; "jujube" are lips or fingers; "hailstones" are teeth.

عاقَبْتُ عَيْني بالدَّمْع والسَّهَر
إذْ فازَ قَلْبي عَلَيْك مِنْ بَصَري
وٱحْتَمَلَتْ ذاكَ وَهْيَ رابحَةٌ
فيكَ وَفازَتْ بلَذَّةِ النَّظَرِ
إبن المعتزّ

I punished my eyes
with tears and sleeplessness
when my heart became jealous
of my eyes
over you
My eyes endured that,
won you over,
and gained the pleasue
of seeing you

Ibn al-Muʿtazz (d. 296/908)

بَكَتْ للفِراقِ وقد راعَها
بُكاءُ الحَبيبِ لِبُعْد الدِّيارْ
كأَنَّ الدُّمُوعَ على خَدِّها
بَقِيَّةُ طَلٍّ على جُلَّنارْ
النّاشِئُ الأَكْبَر أَبو العبَّاس
عبد الله بن محمَّد الأَنْباري

She wept over separation,
frightened by the crying
of the beloved
for the vast distance
between them,
It was as though the tears
on her cheeks
were the remnant of dew
on pomegranate blossoms

al-Nāshiʾ al-Akbar, Abū ʾl-ʿAbbās ʿAbdallah ibn Muḥammad al-Anbārī (d. 293/905)

كأَنَّ تِلْكَ الدُّموعَ قَطْرُ نَدًى
يَقْطُرُ من نَرْجِسٍ على وَرْدِ
إبن الرومي

It was as though her tears
were drops of dew
dripping from narcissus
over roses

Ibn al-Rūmī (d. 283/896)

لَوْلا العُيونُ وَتُفَّاحُ الخُدودِ إِذًا
ما كانَ يَحْسُدُ أَعْمى مَنْ لَهُ نَظَرُ
أَبو تمَّام

Had it not been for eyes
and apple-cheeks
no blind man would ever envy
a person who sees*

Abū Tammām (d. 231/845)

The last two lines can also be read as: A person who sees/ would never envy/ a blind man.

تَبْكي فَتَذْري الدَّمْعَ مِنْ نَرْجِس
وَتَلْطِمُ الوَرْدَ بِعُنَّاب
أَبو نُواس

She cries,
scattering pearls
from narcissus
and striking roses
with jujube

Abū Nuwās (d.198/814)

Carpe Diem

أَقولُ لِصاحِبي وَالْعِيسُ تَهْوي
بِنا بَيْنَ المُنيفةِ فَالضِّمارِ
تَمَتَّعْ مِنْ شَمِيمِ عَرارِ نَجْدٍ
فَما بَعْدَ العَشِيَّةِ مِنْ عَرارِ
لأحدهم

I say to my companion,
while our camels
are swiftly advancing
from Munīfah to Ḍimār:
Enjoy the sweet scent
of the ox-eye plant of Najd
For there will be no ox-eye
after this nightfall

Anonymous (ancient)
Munīfah is a place name, but also means an overtopping of a mountain.
Cf. Robert Herrick's (1591–1674) opening lines of the poem: "To the Virgins, to Make Much of Time:"

Gather ye rosebuds while ye may,
Old time is still a-flying:
And this same flower that smiles to-day
To-morrow will be dying.

ما العَيْشُ إلاَّ سَماعُ مُحْصِنة
وَقَهْوَةٌ تَتْرُكُ الفَتى ثَمِلا
لا أَرْتَجي الحُورَ في الخُلودِ وَهَلْ
يَأْمَلُ حُورَ الجِنانِ مَنْ عَقَلا!
الوليد بن يزيد (الخليفة)

There is no true joy
but lending ear to music,
Or wine that leaves one sunk
in stupor dense,
Houris in Paradise I do not look for:
Does any man of sense?

The Caliph al-Walīd II (d.126 or 127/ 743 or744)
Translated by R. A. Nicholson in *A Literary History of the Arabs*, p. 206.

On Poetry and Meaning

تَغايَرَ الشِّعْرُ فيهِ – إذْ سَهِرْتُ لَهُ –
حَتَّى حَسِبْتُ قَوافيهِ سَتَقْتَتِلُ
أبو تمَّام

Such jealousy has seized
this poetry,
for I have spent many
a watchful night upon it,
that methought each rhyme
would murder the other

Abū Tammām (d. 231/845)

British translation.

فَصُرْتُ أَذَلَّ مِنْ مَعْنًى دَقيق
بِهِ فَقْرٌ إِلى فَهْمٍ جَليلِ
أبو تمَّام

I have become more humble
than a subtle meaning
beseeching sublime
understanding

Abū Tammām (d. 231/845)

وَالشِّعْرُ لَمْحٌ تَكْفي إشارتُهُ
وَلَيْسَ بِالْهَذْرِ طُوِّلَتْ خُطُبُهْ
البحتري

Poetry is but allusion,
suffice it to intimate,
Poetry is not prattle
or long oration

al-Buḥturī (d.284/897)

وَلَوْ كانَ يَفْنى الشِّعْرُ أَفْناهُ ما قَرَتْ
حِياضُكَ مِنْهُ في السِّنينِ الذَّواهِبِ
وَلَكِنَّهُ صَوْبُ العُقولِ إذا ٱنْجَلَتْ
سَحائِبُ مِنْهُ أُعْقِبَتْ بِسَحائِبِ
أبو تمَّام

If poetry were perishable,
poetry sung in praise
of your generosity*,
in years past,
would have exhausted it
But poetry is the rain clouds
of the mind
When such clouds dissipate
others will follow behind

Abū Tammām (d. 231/845)

* *Lit.* collected in your watering troughs.

وَالشِّعْرُ نارٌ بِلا دُخانٍ
وَلِلْقَوافي رُقًى لَطِيفَه
لَوْ هُجِيَ المِسْكُ وَهْوَ أَهْلٌ
لِكُلِّ مَدْحٍ لَصارَ جِيفَه
كَمْ مِنْ ثَقِيلِ المَحَلِّ سامٍ
هَوَتْ بِهِ أَحْرُفٌ خَفِيفَه
ابن سُكَّرَة

Poetry is fire without smoke
and rhymes are subtle spells
Were musk, worthy of all praise,
to be satirized by poetry,
it would become a corpse
How many a noble person
of high stature
has been felled
by light-hearted
verse!

Ibn Sukkarah (d. 385/995)

These lines were noted for the "elixir" of "*ṣanʿah*" (artificial; mannered) poetry. They were cited as a sample of the transformational power of poetry.

فَكَأَنَّما هِيَ في السَّماعِ جَنادِلٌ
وَكَأَنَّما هِيَ في القُلوبِ كَواكِبُ
أبو تمَّام

It is as though my poems
were boulders
in the ears
and stars
in the minds

Abū Tammām (d. 231/845)

On Grief

أَيا شَجَرَ الخابُورِ ما لَكَ مُورِقًا
كَأَنَّكَ لَمْ تَجْزَعْ عَلى ٱبْنِ طَرِيفِ
ليلى بنت طريف الخارجيَّة

But why bud ye, O elder-tree,
with leaves afresh?
Methinks ye have never mourned
Ṭarīf's son, my brother

Laylā bint Ṭarīf al-Khārijiyyah (n.d.)

Translated by R. A. Nicholson in *Translations of Eastern Poetry and Prose*, p. 36.

بِيَوْمٍ كَطُولِ الدَّهْرِ في عَرْضِ مِثْلِه
وَوَجْدِيَ مِنْ هَذا وَهَذاكَ أَطْوَلُ
أَبو تمَّام

Many a day
the length and width
of time
But my grief is longer
than both

Abū Tammām (d. 231/845)

وَقالُوا: أَتَبْكي كُلَّ قَبْرٍ رَأَيْتَهُ
لِقَبْرٍ ثَوى بَيْنَ اللِّوى وَالدَّكادِكِ؟
فَقُلْتُ لَهُمْ: إِنَّ الأَسى يَبْعَثُ الأَسى
دَعُوني! فَهَذا كُلُّهُ قَبْرُ مالِكِ
مُتَمِّم بن نُوَيْرَة

They said: must you weep
over every grave you see
for a grave that lies
between Liwā and Dakādik?
I said: verily, sorrow evokes sorrow
So let me be!
Every grave
is a grave of Mālik

Mutammim ibn Nuwayrah (n.d.)

Mālik was the poet's brother.

أَيُنْكِرُ خَدِّي دُمُوعي وَقَدْ
جَرَتْ مِنْهُ في مَسْلَكٍ سابِلِ
كَأَنَّ الجُفونَ عَلى مُقْلَتي
ثِيابٌ شُقِقْنَ عَلى ثاكِلِ
المتنبِّي

Can my cheeks disown my tears
after they have streamed down
a much traveled course?
It was as though my eyelids
over my eyes
were like the torn garment
of a bereaved mother

al-Mutanabbī (d. 354/965)
A bereaved mother used to tear the front of her garment as a sign of mourning for her child.

On Awe

وَأَخَفْتَ أَهْلَ الشِّرْكِ حَتَّى إِنَّهُ
لَتَخافُكَ النُّطَفُ الّتي لَمْ تُخْلَقِ
أَبو نُواس

You have so frightened
the polytheists
that even their unborn embryos
are afraid of you

Abū Nuwās (d. 198/814)

فَقَدْ بَثَّ عَبْدُ اللهِ خَوْفَ ٱنْتِقامِهِ
عَلَى اللَّيْلِ حَتَّى ما تَدِبُّ عَقارِبُهْ
أَبو تمَّام

Abdullah has spread fear
of his vengeance
over the night
so that scorpions
would not dare to crawl
at night

Abū Tammām (d. 231/845)

يَتَقارَضُونَ إِذا الْتَقَوْا في مَوْطِنٍ
نَظَراً يُزِيلُ مَواطِئَ الأَقْدام
لأَحدهم

They trade,
whenever and wherever they meet,
stares that obliterate
the prints
of each others' feet

Anonymous

يُغْضِي حَياءً وَيُغْضَى مِنْ مَهابَتِه
فَما يُكَلَّمُ إِلاَّ حِينَ يَبْتَسِمُ
الحزين الكِناني

He casts down his eyes
in modesty
Others cast down theirs
in awe
So he can be spoken to
only when he is
smiling

al-Ḥazīn al-Kinānī (n.d.)

فَإِنَّكَ كَاللَّيْلِ الَّذي هُوَ مُدْرِكِي
وَإِنْ خِلْتُ أَنَّ المُنْتَأى عَنْكَ واسِعُ
النابغة

Verily, you are like the night
that will always
overtake me
even if I imagine the distance
between us
to be very vast indeed

al-Nābighah (d. 604 A.D.)

The critic ʿAbd al-Qāhir al-Jurjānī (d. 471/1078) likens this line and one other to "pearls in their shells that do not expose themselves unless you split the shells, or like a beloved that does not show you her face unless you seek her permission."

وَعَلى عَدُوِّكَ، يا ٱبْنَ عَمِّ مُحَمَّدٍ،
رَصَدانِ: ضَوْءُ الصُّبْحِ والإِظْلامُ
فَإِذا تَنَبَّهَ رُعْتَهُ، وَإِذا غَفا
سَلَّتْ عَلَيْهِ سُيُوفَكَ الأَحْلامُ
أَشْجَع السُّلَمي

You have cast over your enemy,
O son of Muhammad,
two spells:
morning light and darkness
If he is awake
you frighten him
and if he is asleep
dreams unsheathe your swords
against him

Ashjaʿ al-Sulamī (d. 195/ 810)

Pressed by the Caliph Hārūn al-Rashīd (reigned from 170–193/ 786–809) as to the origin of the line, the poet Ashjaʿ admitted that he had plagiarized al-Nābighah's line, immediately above.

On Separation

ولا تَحْسَبَنَّ الْحُزْنَ يَبْقى فَإنَّهُ
شِهابُ حَرِيقٍ واقِدٌ ثُمَّ خامِدُ
سَتَأْلَفُ فُقْدانَ الّذي قَدْ فَقَدْتَهُ
كَإِلْفِكَ وُجْدانَ الّذي أَنْتَ واجِدُ
لأَحدهم

Think not that grief lasts forever!
Grief is but a flame
that blazes, then subsides
You will become accustomed
to losing those
you have been separated from
just as you become used
to those around you

Anonymous

قَضِيبُ الكَرْمِ نَقْطَعُهُ فَيَبْكي
ولا نَبْكي إِذا قَطَعَ الحَبِيبُ
الشِّبْلي

We break off a twig
of a grapevine
and it weeps
But we do not shed tears
when the beloved breaks
with us

al-Shiblī (n.d.)

لا تَرْكُنَنَّ إلى الْفِراقِ
وإنْ سَكَنْتَ إلى الْعِناقِ
فَالشَّمْسُ عِنْدَ غُرُوبِها
تَصْفَرُّ مِنْ فَرَقِ الْفِراقِ
أبو العبَّاس الضَّبِّي

Trust not separation
even if you trust in union
Indeed, the sun turns pale
at sunset
for fear
of separation.

Abū 'l-ʿAbbās al-Ḍabbī (n.d.)

تَغَيَّبْتُ كَي لا تَجْتَويني دِيارُكُمْ
ولَوْ لَمْ تَغِبْ شَمْسُ النَّهارِ لَمُلَّت
كُثَيِّر عَزّة

I absented myself
so your tribe would not
dislike me
And if the sun did not set
every day
It would indeed
be boring

Kuthayyir ʿAzzah (d.105/723)

On Jealousy

أَغارُ عَلَيْكِ مِنْ عَيْني ومِنّي
وَمِنْكِ وَمِنْ زَمانِكِ وَالمَكانِ
وَإِنّيَ لَوْ خَبَأْتُكِ في عُيوني
إِلى يَوْمِ القِيامَةِ ما كَفاني
ابن زيدون في ولاّدة

I am jealous over you
of my eyes
of myself
of you
of your time and place
Were I to hide you in my eyes
till the day of judgment
it would still not be enough
for me

Ibn Wallādah Or Ibn Zaydūn under the name Wallādah bint al-Mustakfī (d. 463/1070)

وَحارَبَني فيهِ رَيْبُ الزَّمانِ
كَأَنَّ الزَّمانَ لَهُ عاشِقُ
محمَّد بن وهيب

Vicissitudes of time
have fought with me
over him
It is as though time
were in love
with him

Muḥammad ibn Wahīb (Wuhayb) (n.d.)

ألرِّيحُ تَحْسِدُني عَلَيْكِ
وَلَمْ أَخَلْها في العِدا
لَمَّا هَمَمْتُ بِقُبْلَةٍ
رَدَّتْ عَلى الوَجْهِ الرِّدا
إبراهيم الصولي

The wind is jealous of me
over you
I never thought the wind
was my enemy
When I was about to kiss her
the wind re-veiled her face
swiftly

Ibrāhīm al-Ṣūlī (d. 243/857)

On Homeleaving

وَطُولُ مُقامِ المَرْءِ بِالحَيِّ مُخْلِقٌ
لِدِيباجَتَيْهِ فَاغْتَرِبْ تَتَجَدَّدِ
فَإِنِّي رَأَيْتُ الشَّمْسَ زادَتْ مَحَبَّةً
إِلى النّاسِ أَنْ لَيْسَتْ عَلَيْهِمْ بِسَرْمَدِ

أبو تمّام

Long abiding at one's home(land)
wears out one's youth*
So emigrate, rejuvenate!
Verily, people love the sun more
simply because it is not
always there

Abū Tammām (d. 231/845)

* *Lit.* "cheeks"

حُبُّكَ الأَوْطانَ عَجْزٌ ظاهِرٌ
فَٱغْتَرِبْ تَلْقَ عَنِ الأَهْلِ بَدَلْ
فَبِمُكْثِ الماءِ يَبْقَى آسِنًا
وَسُرى البَدْرِ بِهِ البَدْرُ ٱكْتَمَلْ
لاميَّة ابن الوردي

Love of homeland
is a glaring weakness
So emigrate, and you shall find
a substitute for family
Verily, water is brackish
because it stays still
And the moon becomes full
only because it traverses
the sky

Zayn al-Dīn ʿUmar Ibn al-Wardī (d. 749/1348)
(From his famous Lāmiyyah)

On Longing for First Love, First Home

نَقِّلْ فُؤَادَكَ حَيْثُ شِئْتَ مِنَ الهَوى
ما الحُبُّ إلاَّ لِلْحَبيبِ الأَوَّلِ
كَمْ مَنْزِلٍ في الأَرْضِ يَأْلَفُهُ الفَتى
وَحَنينُهُ أَبَدًا لأَوَّلِ مَنْزِلِ
أبو تمَّام

Let your heart wander
from love to love
everywhere
The only true love
is your first love
Many a place on earth
one calls home,
But one's longing
is forever
for his first home

Abū Tammām (d. 231/845)

لَبَيْتٌ تَخْفِقُ الأَرْواحُ فيهِ
أَحَبُّ إِلَيَّ مِنْ قَصْرٍ مُنيفِ
وَلُبْسُ عَباءَةٍ وَتَقَرُّ عَيْني
أَحَبُّ إِلَيَّ مِنْ لُبْسِ الشُّفوفِ
وَأَكْلُ كُسَيْرَةٍ مِنْ كِسْرِ بَيْتي
أَحَبُّ إِلَيَّ مِنْ أَكْلِ الرَّغيفِ
وَأَصْواتُ الرِّياحِ بِكُلِّ فَجٍّ
أَحَبُّ إِلَيَّ مِنْ نَقْرِ الدُّفوفِ
وَكَلْبٌ يَنْبَحُ الطُّرَّاقَ دُوني
أَحَبُّ إِلَيَّ مِنْ قِطٍّ أَليفِ
وَخِرْقٌ مِنْ بَني عَمِّي نَحيفٌ
أَحَبُّ إِلَيَّ مِنْ عِلْجٍ عَنوفِ
خُشُونَةُ عِيْشَتي في البَدْوِ أَشْهى
إِلى نَفْسي مِنَ العَيْشِ الظَّريفِ
فَما أَبْغي سِوى وَطَني بَديلاً
فَحَسْبي ذاكَ مِنْ وَطَنٍ شَريفِ
ميسون بنت بَحْدل (زوجة الخليفة الأُمويِّ معاوية)

A tent with rustling breezes cool
delights me more than palace high,
And more the cloak of simple wool
than robes in which I learned to sigh.

The crust I ate beside my tent
was more than this fine bread to me;
The wind's voice where the hill-path went
was more than tambourine can be.

And more than purr of friendly cat
I love the watch-dog's bark to hear;
And more than any lubbard fat
I love a Bedouin cavalier.

A harsh life among the Bedouin
is more covetous to me
than all fine living here

All I wish for is my Bedouin home,
Suffice to me
my noble Bedouin home

Maysūn bint Baḥdal (d. ca. 80/700), wife of the caliph Muʿāwiyah ibn Abī Sufyān, the founder of the Umayyad caliphate (d. 60/680).

The first six Arabic lines (the first twelve English couplets) were translated by R.A. Nicholson in *A Literary History of the Arabs*, p. 195. The last English fragment is my translation of the last two Arabic lines.

وَما ذَنْبُ أَعْرابيَّة قَذَفَتْ بها
صُروفُ النَّوى مِنْ حَيْثُ لَمْ تَكُ ظَنَّتِ
تَمَنَّتْ أَحاديثَ الرُّعاةِ وَخَيْمَةً
بِنَجْدٍ فَلَمْ يُقْدَرْ لَها ما تَمَنَّتِ
إِذا ذَكَرَتْ ماءَ العُذَيْبِ وَطِيبَه
وَبَرْدَ حَصاهُ آخرَ اللَّيْلِ حَنَّتِ
لَها أَنَّةٌ عِنْدَ العَشِيِّ وَأَنَّةٌ
سُحَيْراً وَلَوْلا أَنَّتاها لَجُنَّتِ
لأَحدهم

What fault is it
of a Bedouin woman
flung about unawares
by the misfortune of separation
She wished for shepherds' talk
and a tent in Najd
but what she hoped for
did not come to be
Whenever she remembered
the sweet water of al-ʿUdhayb
and its cool pebbles,
at the end of night,
she would pine for it
She groans at nightfall
She moans at daybreak
Were it not for her laments
she would have gone mad

Anonymous

أَيُّها الرَّاكِبُ المُيَمِّمُ أَرْضي
أَقْرِ مِنْ بَعْضِيَ السَّلامَ لِبَعْضِ
إِنَّ جِسْمي كَما عَلِمْتَ بِأَرْضٍ
وَفُؤَادي وَمالِكيهِ بِأَرْضِ
قَدَّرَ البَيْنُ بَيْنَنا فَافْتَرَقْنا
وَطَوى البَيْنُ عَنْ جُفوني غَمْضي
قَدْ قَضى اللهُ بِالفِراقِ عَلَيْنا
فَعَسى بِاجْتِماعِنا سَوْفَ يَقْضي
عبد الرحمن بن معاوية (عبد الرحمن الداخل)

O traveler, wending your way
towards my homeland,
give my greetings to my kin,
My body, as you know, is in one land
but my heart and those who own it
are in another
Fate has decreed that we part
and has deprived my eyes of sleep
God has decreed that we separate
May He decree that again
we meet

'Abd al-Raḥmān al-Dākhil ('Abd al-Raḥmān ibn Muʿāwiyah) d. 172/788), founder of the Umayyad dynasty in al-Andalus (Spain).

تَبَدَّتْ لَنا وَسْطَ الرُّصافةِ نَخْلةٌ
تَناءَتْ بِأَرْضِ الغَرْبِ عَنْ بَلَدِ النَّخْلِ
فَقُلْتُ: شَبِيهي في التَّغَرُّبِ والنَّوى
وَطُولِ التَّنائِي عَنْ بَنِيَّ وَعَنْ أَهْلي
نَشَأْتِ بِأَرْضٍ أَنْتِ فيها غَريبةٌ
فَمِثْلُكِ في الإِقْصاءِ وَالمُنْتَأَى مِثْلي
سَقَتْكِ غَوادي المُزْنِ مِنْ صَوْبِها الّذي
يَسِحُّ وَيَسْتَمْرِي السِّماكَيْنِ بِالوَبْلِ
عبد الرحمن الداخل

A palm tree I beheld
in the middle of al-Ruṣāfah
A tree alone in the West
remote from the land of palm trees
and I said to it:
Like me, you are in exile
and long separation
from kin and family
You have grown a stranger
in a foreign land
displaced like me
and far far away from home
May the morning clouds water you
and may abundant rain
forever comfort you

ʿAbd al-Raḥmān al-Dākhil, d. 172/788)

يا نَخْلَ، أَنْتِ غَريبةٌ مِثْلي
في الغَرْبِ نائيةٌ عَنِ الأَصْلِ
فَابْكِي وَهَلْ تَبْكي مُكَمَّمةٌ
عَجْماءُ لَمْ تُطْبَعْ على خَتْلِ؟
لَوْ أَنَّها تَبْكي إذًا لَبَكَتْ
ماءَ الفُراتِ وَمَنْبتَ النَّخْلِ
لَكِنَّها ذَهِلَتْ وأَذْهَلَني
بُغْضي بَني العَبّاسِ عَنْ أَهْلي
عبد الرحمن الداخل

O Palm, thou art a stranger in the West
Far from thy Orient home, like me unblest.
Weep! But thou canst not. Dumb, dejected tree
Thou art not made to sympathise with me.
Ah, thou wouldst weep, if thou hadst tears to pour,
For thy companions on Euphrates' shore;
But yonder tall groves thou rememberest not,
As I, in hating foes,* have my old friends forgot.

ʿAbd al-Raḥmān al-Dākhil (d. 172/ 788)

Translated by R.A. Nicholson in *A Literary History of the Arabs*, p. 418.

* The "foes" of ʿAbd al-Raḥmān al-Dākhil are "Banū 'l -ʿAbbās" (the Abbasids). The Abbasid Caliphate in Baghdad extended between 750 and 1258 A.D.

On Noble Descent

أَضاءَتْ لَهُمْ أَحْسابُهُمْ وَوُجُوهُهُمْ
دُجى اللَّيْلِ حَتَّى نَظَّمَ الجَزْعَ ثاقِبُهْ
أبو الطَّحمان القَيْنِي

Their faces and noble descent
have so illuminated
the dark night
that a piercer of beads
could string his onyx

Abū 'l-Ṭaḥmān al-Qaynī (died in the year 10 before Hijrah, i.e., 611??)

فَتًى لَوْ يُنادِي الشَّمْسَ أَلْقَتْ قِناعَها
أَوِ القَمَرَ السَّارِي لَأَلْقى المَقالِدا
الأَعشى

What a noble youth he is!
Were he to sit
in company with* the sun
it would cast away its veil,
Or in company with the moon
the moon would drop
its reins

al-Aʿshā (d. 8/629)

* 'To sit in company with' "*yunādī*" also means to call, to summon or to vie in glory with.

On Transcendent Qualities

فَإِنْ تَفُقِ الأَنَامَ وَأَنْتَ مِنْهُمْ
فَإِنَّ الْمِسْكَ بَعْضُ دَمِ الغَزَالِ
المتنبِّي

You surpass mankind,
yet you are human,
just as musk is part
of the blood
of a gazelle

al-Mutanabbī (d. 354/965)

تَتَقاصَرُ الأَفْهَامُ عَنْ إِدْراكه
مِثْلُ الّذي الأَفْلاكُ فِيهِ وَالدُّنَا
المتنبِّي

Minds fall short
of comprehending him
just as they fail to comprehend
the worlds
and celestial spheres

al-Mutanabbī (d. 354/965)

لَوِ الْفَلَكُ الدَّوَّارُ أَبْغَضْتَ سَيْرَهُ
لَعَوَّقَهُ شَيْءٌ عَنِ الدَّوَرانِ
المتنبِّي

Were you to loathe the journeying
of the celestial sphere
something would hinder
its journeying

al-Mutanabbī (d. 354/965)

عَدُوُّكَ مَذْمُومٌ بِكُلِّ لِسَانِ
وَلَوْ كانَ مِنْ أَعْدائِكَ القَمَرانِ
المتنبِّي

Your foes are defamed
by every tongue
even if the sun and moon
are among
your foes

al-Mutanabbī (d. 354/965)

كَأَنِّي دَحَوْتُ الأَرْضَ مِنْ خِبْرَتِي بِها
كَأَنِّي بَنَى الإِسْكَنْدَرُ السَّدَّ مِنْ عَزْمِي
المتنبِّي

It was as if I had flattened the earth
with my experience
And Alexander had built the dam
with my might

Al-Mutanabbī (d. 354/965)

وَأَنَا الْمَنِيَّةُ في المَواطِنِ كُلِّها
وَالطَّعْنُ مِنِّي سَابِقُ الآجال

عنترة بن شدَّاد

I am death on all battlefields
and my lance-thrusting
precedes predestined
fates

    'Antarah ibn Shaddād (d.615 A.D.)

إِذا ما غَضِبْنا غَضْبَةً مُضَرِيَّةً
هَتَكْنا حِجابَ الشَّمْسِ أَوْ قَطَرَتْ دَما

بشَّار بن بُرْد

Were we to have a Muḍarī rage
we would rend the veil
of the sun*
and the sun would drip
    precious blood

    Bashshār ibn Burd (d. 167/784)

---

* The sun's veil is its light; but the veil-image here refers to the dust clouds of the battlefield. Muḍarī refers to the tribe of Muḍarīyah.

On Death Transformed

كَذا فَلْيَجِلَّ الْخَطْبُ وَلْيَفْدَحِ الأَمْرُ
فَلَيْسَ لِعَيْنٍ لَمْ يَفِضْ مَاؤُهَا عُذْرُ
تُوُفِّيَتِ الآمَالُ بَعْدَ مُحَمَّدٍ
وَأَصْبَحَ في شُغْلٍ عَنِ السَّفَرِ السَّفْرُ
فَأَثْبَتَ في مُسْتَنْقَعِ الْمَوْتِ رِجْلَهُ
وَقالَ لَهَا: مِنْ تَحْتِ أَخْمُصِكِ الْحَشْرُ
أبو تمَّام

So be it!
Let the grave calamity
and momentous misfortune
be felt
Eyes whose waters
have not gushed forth
have no reason to exist
Hopes are dead
after Muḥammad's death
and travellers from travel
are distracted

...

He steadied his foot
in the swamp of death
and said to it:
resurrection lies

under the hollow
of your sole

Abū Tammām (d. 231/845)

From a famous elegiac poem on Muḥammad ibn Ḥumayd (Ḥamīd) al-Ṭūsī, the poet's friend and patron.

عُلُوٌّ في الْحَيَاةِ وَفي الْمَمَاتِ
بِحَقٍّ أَنْتَ إِحْدَى الْمُعْجِزاتِ
كَأَنَّ النَّاسَ حَوْلَكَ حِينَ قَامُوا
وُفُودُ نَدَاكَ أَيَّامَ الصِّلاتِ
كَأَنَّكَ وَاقِفٌ فِيهِمْ خَطِيبًا
وَكُلُّهُمُ قِيَامٌ لِلصَّلاةِ
مَدَدْتَ يَدَيْكَ نَحْوَهُمُ ٱحْتِفاءً
كَمَدِّهِما إِلَيْهِمْ بِالْهِبَاتِ
وَلَمَّا ضَاقَ بَطْنُ الأَرْضِ عَنْ أَنْ
يَضُمَّ عُلاكَ مِنْ بَعْدِ الْمَمَاتِ
أَصَارُوا الْجَوَّ قَبْرَكَ وَٱسْتَنَابُوا
عَنِ الأَكْفانِ ثَوْبَ السَّافِيَاتِ
أبو الحسن الأنباري

Elevated in life and in death!
You are truly one
of life's miracles
It is as though the people
around you,
as they stood,
were seekers of your largesse
on the days
of free giving
It is as though you have arisen,
a preacher among them,
and they have risen for prayer
You stretched out your hands
towards them
in welcome

as you had extended them
in giving
Since the bowels of the earth
were too strait
to contain your grandeur
after death
they made the sky your grave
and replaced shrouds
with the raiment
of dusty winds

Ibn al-Anbārī (4th century AH/10th century AD)

These are the opening lines of an elegiac poem by Ibn al-Anbārī in which he elegizes the vizier Ibn Baqiyyah, the poet's patron and friend, who was trampled to death by elephants for giving a bad war advice to the ruler ʿIzza al-Dawlah (d. 267…..). The ruler had his body crucified and left hanging in the center of Baghdad for days. Ibn al-Anbārī composed this splendid poem without mention of crucifixion in it

On Battle, Battlefields, and Swords

وَنَبَّالَةٍ مِنْ بُحْتُرٍ لَوْ تَعَمَّدُوا
بِلَيْلٍ أَناسِيَّ النَّواظِرِ لَمْ يُخْطُوا
أبو العلاء المعرِّي

If, even at night,
the archers of Buḥtur
were to aim at the pupils
of their enemies' eyes,
they would not miss

Abū 'l-ʿAlā' al-Maʿarrī (d. 449/1057)

ولا عَيْبَ فِيهِمْ غَيْرَ أَنَّ سُيُوفَهُمْ
بِهِنَّ فُلُولٌ مِنْ قِراعِ الكَتائِبِ
النابغة الذُّبْياني

There is no fault in them
except that their sword blades
are notched
from striking
    mailed squadrons

al-Nābighah al-Dhubyānī (d. 604 A.D.)

صَبَبْنا عَلَيْهِمْ ظالِمينَ سِياطَنا
وَطَارَتْ بِها أَيْدٍ سِراعٌ وَأَرْجُلُ
ابن المُعتزّ

We lashed our whips harshly
on our horses
until their swift fore
and hind legs
flew away
    with them

Ibn al-Muʿtazz (d. 296/908)

كَأَنَّ مُثَارَ النَّقْعِ فَوْقَ رُؤُوْسِنَا
وَأَسْيَافَنَا لَيْلٌ تَهَاوَى كَوَاكِبُهْ
بشّار بن بُرْد

It was as if the dust
of the battlefield
raised over our heads,
and our swords,
had been a night
and its falling
    stars

Bashshār ibn Burd (d. 167/784)

عَجَاجًا تَعْثُرُ العِقْبانُ فيهِ
كَأَنَّ الجَوَّ وَعْثٌ أَوْ خَبارُ
المتنبِّي

Eagles stumble in the dust
of the battlefield
as if the sky
were flat ground
or soft soil

al-Mutanabbī (d. 354/965)

فَلَوْلا الرِّيحُ أُسْمِعَ أَهْلُ حُجْرٍ
صَلِيلَ البِيضِ تُقْرَعُ بِالذُّكُورِ
المُهَلْهِل

Had it not been for the wind
the people of Ḥujr
would have heard
the clanking of helmets
struck by sharp
swords

al-Muhalhil (d. ca. 531 A.D.)

وَيَهْتَزُّ مِثْلَ السَّيْفِ لَوْ لَمْ تَسُلَّهُ
يَدَانِ لَسَلَّتْهُ ظُبَاهُ مِنَ الغِمْدِ
أبو تمَّام

It quivers like a sword
that, if it were not drawn
by the swordsman's hand,
its sharp edge alone
would unsheathe it

Abū Tammām (d. 231/845)

وَجَنَيْتُمُ ثَمَرَ الوَقَائِعِ يَانِعًا
بِالنَّصْرِ مِنْ وَرَقِ الحَدِيدِ الأَخْضَرِ
أبو القاسم بن هانئ (أندلسيّ)

You have reaped
the ripe fruits of battle
with the verdant leaves
of green iron*

Abū 'l-Qāsim ibn Hānī' (Andalusian poet, d. 362/972)

* This line on bravery on the battlefield was cited as an example of a novel and excellent meaning. See *The Neckveins of Winter*, p, 47

لَنَا الجَفَنَاتُ الغُرُّ يَلْمَعْنَ في الضُّحَى
وَأَسْيافُنا يَقْطُرْنَ مِنْ نَجْدَةٍ دَمَا
حسَّان بن ثابت

Our white porringers
glitter in the forenoon
And our swords,
because of our courage
in rushing to the aid
of others,
drip precious
blood

Ḥassān ibn Thābit (d. 55/674)

On Flora, Fauna, and Nature

كَأَنَّ قُلُوبَ الطَّيْرِ رَطْبًا وَيَابِسًا
لَدَى وَكْرِها العُنَّابُ والحَشَفُ الْبَالِي
امْرؤ القَيس

It is as though the fresh
and desiccated hearts
of birds,
in their aerie,
were jujube
and overripe dates

Imru' al-Qays (d. 545 A.D.)

كَأَنَّ عُيُونَ الوَحْشِ حَوْلَ خِبَائِنا
وَأَرْحُلِنا الْجَزْعُ الّذي لَمْ يُثَقَّبِ
امْرؤ القَيس

It is as though the eyes
of beasts
around our saddles
and tents
were un-bored onyx

Imru' al-Qays (d. 545 A.D.)

نَظَرْتُ إِلَيْها وَالنُّجومُ كَأَنَّها
مَصَابِيحُ رُهْبانٍ تُشَبُّ لِقُفَّالِ
امْرؤ القَيس

It is as though the stars,
when I stared
at the sky,
were monks' lanterns
lit for homecomers

Imru' al-Qays (d. 545 A.D.)

The three lines, above, of Imru' al-Qays were cited as a superb example of the excellent employment of simile, where two objects in each line are accurately compared in image and form.

أَتَاكَ الرَّبِيعُ الطَّلْقُ يَخْتَالُ ضَاحِكًا
مِنَ الحُسْنِ حَتَّى كادَ أَنْ يَتَكَلَّما
البُحْتُري

Cheerful spring has come!
Strutting about
laughing with beauty
so it could almost
talk

al-Buḥturī (d. 284/897)

وَلَمَّا قَضَيْنا مِنْ مِنًى كُلَّ حَاجَةٍ
وَمَسَّحَ بِالأَرْكَانِ مَنْ هُوَ مَاسِحُ
وَشُدَّتْ عَلى حُدْبِ المَهارِي رِحَالُنَا
ولا يَنْظُرُ الغَادِي الّذي هُوَ رَائِحُ
أَخَذْنا بِأَطْرافِ الأَحَادِيث بَيْنَنا
وَسَالَتْ بِأَعْنَاقِ المَطِيِّ الأَبَاطِحُ
كُثَيِّر عَزَّة

When we had performed our duties at Minā
and whoever wished to touch the arkān*
had done so
And when our saddlebags had been strapped
to the humpbacked dromedaries,
and the early comer would not notice
the late comer
We began to exchange
tidbits of conversation
while the ravines flowed
with the necks
of our mounts

Kuthayyir ʿAzzah (d.105/723)

* "*Arkān*" are the sacred corners of the *Kaʿbah*; "duties at Minā" are part of the religious ceremonial rituals of pilgrimage to Mecca.. These three lines were cited as an example of factual truth that can be transformed metaphorically into poetic truth.

On Physical Attributes

مَنْ رأَى مِثْلَ حِبَّتِي
تُشْبِهُ الْبَدْرُ إِذْ بَدَا
تَدْخُلُ الْيَوْمَ ثُمَّ تَدْخُلُ
أَرْدَافُهَا غَـدَا
المؤمَّل بن أَمْيَل

Who has ever seen anyone
like my beloved
who resembles the full moon
when she appears
If she enters the house today
her buttocks will follow
tomorrow

al-Mu'ammal ibn Amyal (n.d.)

كَأَنَّ عُيُونَ الوَحْشِ حَوْلَ خِبَائِنا
وَأَرْحُلِنا الْجَزْعُ الّذي لَمْ يُثَقَّبِ
امْرؤ القَيس

It is as though
the eyes of beasts
around our saddles and tents
were un-bored onyx

Imru' al-Qays (d. 545 A.D.)

كَأَنَّ قُلُوبَ الطَّيْرِ رَطْبًا وَيَابِسًا
لَدَى وَكْرِهَا العُنَّابُ والحَشَفُ الْبَالِي
امْرؤ القَيس

It is as though the fresh
and desiccated hearts of birds
in their aerie
were jujube
and overripe dates

Imru' al-Qays (d. 545 A.D.)

وَقَصِيرٌ لا تَعْمَلُ الشَّمْسُ
ظِلاًّ لِقَامَتِهْ
يَعْثُرُ النَّاسُ في الطَّرِيقِ
بِهِ مِنْ دَمَامَتِهْ
لشاعر مُحدَث

He is so short
that the sun
does not make a shadow
for him
He is so short and ugly
that people on the road
trip over him

Anonymous

نَظَرْتُ إِلَيْها وَالنُّجُومُ كَأَنَّها
مَصَابِيحُ رُهْبانٍ تُشَبُّ لِقُفَّالِ
امْرؤ القَيس

It is as though the stars
were monks' lanterns
lit for homecomers
when I stared at the sky

Imru' al-Qays (d. 545 A.D.)

The three lines, above, of Imru' al-Qays were cited as a superb example of the excellent employment of simile, where two objects in each line are accurately compared in image and form.

أَت.اَكَ الرَّبِيعُ الطَّلْقُ يَخْتَالُ ضَاحِكًا
مِنَ الحُسْنِ حَتَّى كادَ أَنْ يَتَكَلَّما
البُحْتُري

Cheerful spring has come
strutting about
so laughing with beauty
that it could almost talk

al-Buḥturī (d. 284/897)

وَلَمَّا قَضَيْنا مِنْ مِنًى كُلَّ حَاجَةٍ
وَمَسَّحَ بِالأرْكَانِ مَنْ هُوَ مَاسِحُ
وَشُدَّتْ عَلى حُدْبِ المَهارِي رِحَالُنا
ولا يَنْظُرُ الغَادِي الّذي هُوَ رَائِحُ
أَخَذْنا بِأَطْرافِ الأَحَادِيثِ بَيْنَنا
وَسَالَتْ بِأَعْنَاقِ المَطِيِّ الأَبَاطِحُ
كُثَيِّر عَزَّة

When we had performed our duties at Minā
and whoever wished to touch the arkān*
had done so
And when our saddlebags had been strapped
to the humpbacked dromedaries
and the early comer would not notice
the late comer
We began to exchange
tidbits of conversation
while the ravines flowed
with the necks
of our mounts

Kuthayyir ʿAzzah (d.105/723)

* "*Arkān*" are the sacred corners of the *Kaʿbah*; "duties at Minā" are part of the religious ceremonial rituals of pilgrimage to Mecca.. These three lines were cited as an example of factual truth that can be transformed metaphorically into poetic truth.

Hyperbolic Miscellany

لِي مَنْزِلٌ كَوِجَارِالضَّبِّ أَقْطُنُهُ
ضَنْكٌ تَقَارَبَ قُطْرَاهُ فَقَدْ ضَاقَا
أَرَاهُ قَالَبَ جِسْمِي حِينَ أَنْزِلُهُ
فَلا أَمُدُّ بِهِ رِجْلاً وَلا سَاقَا
لشاعرٍ قديم

I live in a house
as cramped
as a lizard's lair
Its sides are so close
to each other
that indeed it is strait
My house is a mold
for my body
When I am in it
I cannot stretch a leg
or a foot

Anonymous

وَلَوْ أَنَّ بُرْغُوثًا عَلى ظَهْرِ قَمْلَةٍ
يَكُرُّ عَلى صَفَّيْ تَمِيمٍ لَوَلَّتِ
الطِّرِمَّاح

If a flea
on the back of a louse
were to charge
against the ranks of Banū Tamīm
they surely would flee

al-Ṭirimmāḥ (d. ca. 105/723)

The critics asserted that description leading to impossibility or absurdity, as in the above four verses, is palatable only if it is intended for derision, disparagement, or ridicule.

Bibliography

Sources Actually Consulted

Ajami, Mansour. *Al-Marzūqī's Treatment of 'Amūd al-Shi'r*. Ph.D. Diss. Columbia University (1976).

_____. *The Neckveins of Winter: The Controversy over Natural and Artificial Poetry in Medieval Arabic Literary Criticism*. E. J. Brill (Leiden, 1984).

_____. *The Alchemy of Glory: The Dialectic of Truthfulness and Untruthfulness in Medieval Arabic Literary Criticism*. Three Continents Press (Washington, D.C., 1988.

_____. "Death Transformed: A Counter Reading of Crucifixion", in Journal of Arabic Literature, vol. XXI, Part 1, March 1990.

Allen, Roger, *An Introduction to Arabic Literature*, Cambridge University Press (Cambridge, 2000).

Al-Āmidī, Abū 'l-Qāsim al-Ḥasan ibn Bishr, *Al-Muwāzanah Bayn Shi'r Abī Tammām wa-'l-Buḥturī*. Ed. Aḥmad Ṣaqr, 2 vols., Dār al-Ma'ārif (Cairo, 1961, 1965).

Al-'Amīdī, Abū Sa'd Muḥammad ibn Aḥmad, *al-Ibānah* 'an *Sariqāt al-Mutanabbī*. Ed. Ibrahīm al-Dasūqī al-Bisāṭī, Dār al-Ma'ārif (Egypt, 1961).

Arberry, A. J., *The* Seven Odes. George Allen and Unwin Ltd. (London, 1957).

----------, *Poems of al-Mutanabbī: A Selection with Introduction, Translations and Notes*, Cambridge University Press (Cambridge, 1967).

----------, *Arabic Poetry: A Primer for Students*, Camgridge University Press (Cambridge, 1965).

Arisṭūṭālīs (Aristotle), *Fann al-Shidr; ma' al-Tarjamah al-'Arabiyyah al-Qadīmah wa-Shurūḥ al-Fārābī wa-Ibn Sīnā wa-Ibn Rushd*. Tr. and Ed. 'Abd al-Raḥmān Badawī, 2nd ed., Dār al-Thaqāfah (Beirut, 1973).

Al-'Askarī, Abū Hilāl al-Ḥasan ibn 'Abdallah, *Kitab* al-*Ṣinā'atayn —al-Kitābah wa-'l-Shi'r*. Eds. 'Alī Muḥammad al-Bijāwī and Muḥammad Abū 'l-Faḍl Ibrāhīm, 2nd ed. (Cairo, 1971).

Al-Aṣma'ī, Abū Sa'īd 'Abd al-Malik, *Fuḥūlat al-Shu'arā'*. Eds. Muḥammad 'Abd al-Mun'im Khafājī and Ṭāha Muḥammad al-Zaynī (Cairo, 1953).

AL-Badī'ī, Yūsuf, *Al-Ṣubḥ al-Munbīḥ an Ḥaythiyyat al-Mutanabbī*. Eds. Muṣṭafā al-Saqqā, Muḥammad Shatā, 'Abdū Ziādah 'Abdū, Dār al-Ma'ārif (Cairo, 1963).

Beeston, A. F. L., *Selections from the Poetry of Bashshar*, Cambridge University Press (Cambridge, 1977).

Al-Buḥturī, Abū 'Ubādah, *Dīwān al-Buḥturī*. Ed. Ḥasan Kāmil al-Ṣayrafī, Dār al-Ma'ārif, 5 vol. (Cairo, 1963-1978).

Chejne, Anwar G., *Muslim Spain: Its History and Culture*, The University of Minnesota Press (Minneapolis, 1974).

Dāghir, Yūsuf As'ad, *Maṣādir al-Dirāsah al-Adabiyyah*, Vol. 1, 2nd ed. Al-Maṭba'ah al-Mukhalliṣiyyah (Saida, Lebanon, 1961).

Freeman-Grenville, G. S. P., *The Muslim and Christian Calendars*, Oxford University Press (London, 1963).

Gibb, H. A. R., *Arabic Literature—An Introduction*, 2nd revised edition, Oxford University Press (Oxford, 1966).

Grunebaum, Gustave E. von, *A Tenth-Century Document of Arabic Literary Theory and Criticism: The Sections on Poetry of Al-Bāqillānī's I'jāz al-Qur'ān*, Translated and annotated, The University of Chicago Press (Chicago, 1950).

Heinrichs, Wolfhart, *The Hand of the Northwind*. DMG, Kommissionsverlag Franz Steiner GmbH (Wiesbaden, 1977).

Ibn al-Athīr, Ḍiyā' al-Dīn, *Al-Mathal al-Sā'ir fī Adab al-Kātib wa-'l-Shā'ir*. Eds. Aḥmad al-Ḥūfī and Badawī Ṭabānah, Maktabat Nahḍat Miṣr, 4 vols. (Cairo, 1959-1962).

Ibn Khafājah, Ibrāhīm, *Dīwān Ibn Khafājah*. Ed. Muṣṭafā Ghāzī, Dār al-Maʿārif (Alexandria, 1960).

Ibn Khillikān, Aḥmad, *Wafayāt al-Aʿyān wa-Anbā' Abnā' al-Zamān*, Ed. Iḥsān ʿAbbās, Dār Ṣādir, 8 Vols. (Beirut, 1968-1977).

Ibn al-Muʿtazz, ʿAbdallah, *Kitāb al-Badīʿ*. Ed. Ignatius Kratchkovsky, Luzac & Co. (London, 1935).

Ibn Qutaybah, Abū Muḥammad ʿAbdallah ibn Muslim, *Introduction au Livre de la Poesie et des Poetes*. Texte arabe avec introduction, traduction et commentaire par Gaudefroy-Demombynes, "Les Belles Lettres." Association Guillaume Bude (Paris, 1947).

Ibn Rashīq al-Qayrawānī, *Qurāḍat al-Dhahab fī Naqd Ashʿār al-ʿArab*, Ed. Al-Shādhilī Bū Yaḥyā, al-Sharikah al-Tūnisiyyah li-'l-Tawzīʿ (Tunis, 1972).

----------, *Al-ʿUmdah fī Maḥāsin al-Shiʿr wa-Ādābih wa-Naqdih*. Ed. Muḥammad Muḥyiddīn ʿAbd al-Ḥamīd, 4th ed., 2 Vols. Dār al-Jīl (Beirut, 1972).

Ibn Rushd, Abū 'l-Walīd, *Talkhīṣ Kitāb Arisṭūṭālīs fī al-Shiʿr [al-Sharḥ al-Wasīṭ]* in *Fann al-Shiʿr*, Ed. ʿAbd al-Raḥmān Badawī. 2nd. Edn, Dār al-Thaqāfah (Beirut, 1973).

Ibn Sallām al-Jumaḥī, *Ṭabaqāt Fuḥūl al-Shuʿarā'*. Ed. Maḥmūd Muḥammad Shākir (Cairo, 1952).

Ibn Sīnā, Abū ʿAlī al-Ḥusayn ibn ʿAbdallah, *Fann al-Shiʿr min Kitāb al-Shifā'*, in *Atisṭuṭālīs—Fann al-Shiʿr*, Tr. and Ed. ʿAbd al-Raḥmān Badawī, 2nd ed., Dār al-Thaqāfah (Beirut, 1973).

Ibn Ṭabāṭabā, Muḥammad ibn Aḥmad, *ʿIyār al-Shiʿr*. Eds. Ṭaha al-Ḥājirī and Muḥammad Zaghlūl Salām (Cairo, 1956).

Ibn Wahb al-Kātib, Isḥāq ibn Ibrāhīm, *Al-Burhān fī Wujūh al-Bayān*. Eds. Aḥmad Maṭlūb and Khadījah al-Ḥadīthī (Baghdad, 1967).

Ibn Wakīʿ al-Tinnīsī, *Al-Munṣif fī Naqd al-Shiʿr wa-Bayān Sariqāt al-Mutanabbī wa-Mushkil Shiʿrih*. Ed. Muḥammad Raḍwān al-Dāyah (Damascus, 1982).

Irwin, Robert, *Night & Horses & The Desert: An Anthology of Classical Arabic Literature*, Anchor Books (New York, 2002).

Al-Jāḥiẓ, Abū ʿUthmān ʿAmr ibn Baḥr, *al-Bayān wa-'l-Tabyīn*, Ed. ʿAbd al-Salām Muḥammad Harūn, 4 vols, Maktabat al-Khānjī bi-Mi ṣr , 4th ed (Cairo, 1975).

Al-Jurjānī, ʿAbd al-ʿAzīz, *Al-Wasāṭah Bayn al-Mutanabbī wa-Khuṣūmih*. Eds. Muḥammad Abū 'l-Faḍl Ibrāhīm and ʿAlī al-Bijāwī (Cairo, 1966).

Al-Jurjānī, ʿAbd al-Qāhir, *Asrār al-Balāghah*. Ed. Hellmut Ritter, Istanbul Government Press (Istanbul, 1954).

-------------, *Dalā'il al-Iʿjāz*. Ed. Muḥammad ʿAbd al-Munʿim Khafājī, Maktabat al-Qāhirah (Cairo, 1969).

Kaḥḥālah, ʿUmar Riḍā, *Muʿjam al-Mu'allifīn*, Vol. 1 (of 15 vols.), Maṭbaʿat al-Taraqqī (Damascus, 1957-1961).

Al-Khafājī, Ibn Sinān, *Sirr al-Faṣāḥah*. Ed. ʿAbd al-Mutaʿāl al-Ṣaʿīdī, 2nd ed. (Cairo, 1969).

Lyall, Charles James, *Translations of Ancient Arabian Poetry*, Williams And Norgate (London, 1885).

Al-Maʿarrī, Abū 'l-ʿAlā', *Al-Luzūmiyyāt [Luzūm mā lā Yalzam]*. Dār Ṣādir- Dār Beirut (Beirut, 1961).

Al-Majlisī, Muḥammad Bāqir, *Biḥār al-Anwār*, Wizārat al-Irshād al-Islāmī, Vol. 1 (Tehran, 1986).

Al-Marzubānī, Abū ʿAbdallah M. ibn ʿImrān, *Al-Muwashshaḥ*. Ed. ʿAlī Muḥammad al-Bijāwī (Cairo, 1969).

Al-Marzūqī, Abū ʿAlī Aḥmad ibn M. ibn al-Ḥasan, *Sharḥ Dīwān al-Ḥamāsah*. Eds. Aḥmad Amīn and ʿAbd al-Salām Hārūn, 2nd ed. (Cairo, 1967).

Menocal, Maria Rosa, *The Ornament of the World: How Muslims, Jews, and Christians Created a Culture of Tolerance in Medieval Spain*, Back Bay Books/ Little, Brown and Company (New York, 2002).

Al-Mutanabbī, Abū 'l-Tayyib, *Sharḥ Dīwān al-Mutanabbī-- al-ʿArf al-Ṭayyib fī Sharḥ Dīwān Abī 'l-Ṭayyib*, by al-Shaykh Nāṣīf al-Yāzijī, 2 Vols., Dār Ṣādir- Dār Beirut (Beirut, 1964).

Nicholson, R. A., *A Literary History of the Arabs*. Cambridge University Press, reprinted (Cambridge, 1977).

---------------, *Studies in Islamic Poetry*. Cambridge University Press (Cambridge, 1921).

---------------, *Translations of Eastern Poetry and Prose*. Cambridge University Press (Cambridge, 1922).

Nykl, A. R., *Hispano-Arabic Poetry and Its Relations with the Old Provencal Troubadours* (Baltimore, 1946, Reprint 1970).

Al-Qarṭājannī, Ḥāzim, *Minhāj al-Bulaghā' wa-Sirāj al-Udabā'*. Ed. Muḥammad al-Ḥabīb ibn al-Khūjah, Dār al-Kutub al-Sharqiyyah (Tunis, 1966).

Qudāmah ibn Ja'far, *Naqd al=Shi'r*. Ed. S. A. Bonebakker, E. J. Brill (Leiden, 1956).

Al-Rāghib al-Iṣfahānī, *Muḥāḍarāt al-Udabā' wa-Muḥāwarāt al-Shu'arā' wa-'l-Bulaghā'*, 2 Vols. (Cairo, 1908).

Rihani, Ameen, *The Luzumiyat of Abu'l –Ala*, The Sader-Rihani Printing Co., 4th edn (Beirut, 1944).

Sells, Michael A., *Desert Tracings; Six Classic Arabian Odes*, Wesleyan University Press (Middletown, Connecticut, 1989).

Al-Ṣūlī, Abū Bakr Muḥammad ibn Yaḥyā, *Akhbār Abī Tammām*. Eds. Khalīl

Maḥmūd 'Asākir, Muḥammad 'Abdū 'Azzām, Naẓīr al-Islām al-Hindī, Al-Maktab al-Tijārī li-'l-Ṭibā'ah wa-'l-Nashr wa-'l-Tawzī' (Beirut, n.d.).

Al-Ṣūlī, Abū Bakr Muḥammad ibn Yaḥyā, *Akhbār al-Buḥturī*. Ed. Ṣāliḥ al-Ashtar, 2nd ed. Dār al-Fikr (Damascus, 1964).

Tha'lab, Abū 'l-'Abbās Aḥmad ibn Yaḥyā, *Qawā'id al-Shi'r*. Ed. Ramaḍān 'Abd al-Tawwāb (Cairo, 1966).

Al-Tha'ālibī, Abū Manṣūr 'Abd al-Malik ibn Muḥammad ibn Ismā'īl, *Yatīmat al-Dahr fī Shu'arā' Ahl al-'Aṣr*, 2 Vols. Maṭbū'āt al-Maṭba'ah al- Ḥifniyyah (Damascus, n.d.).

Usāmah ibn Munqidh, *al-Badī fī Naqd al-Shi'r*. Eds. A. Aḥmad Badawī and Ḥāmid 'Abd al-Majīd, Al-Idārah al-'Āmmah li-'l-Thaqāfah (Cairo, 1960).

Yāqūt ibn 'Abdallah al-Rūmī al-Ḥamawī, *Mu'jam al-Udabā'* or *Irshād al-Arīb ilā Ma'rifat al-Adīb*, Ed. D. S. Margoliouth, 7 Vols. (London: Luzac, 1923-1931).

Wright, W., A Grammar of the Arabic Language, 3rd edn, Librairie Du Liban (Beirut, 1996).